EVERY PERSON'S
GUIDE TO
SUKKOT, SHEMINI ATZERET, AND SIMCHAT TORAH

EVERY PERSON'S
GUIDE TO
SUKKOT, SHEMINI ATZERET, AND SIMCHAT TORAH

RONALD H. ISAACS

JASON ARONSON INC.
Northvale, New Jersey
Jerusalem

This book was set in 12 pt. ITC Garamond Light by Alabama Book Composition of Deatsville, AL and printed and bound by Book-mart Press, Inc. of North Bergen, NJ.

10   9   8   7   6   5   4   3   2   1

Library of Congress Cataloging-in-Publication Data

Isaacs, Ronald H.
   Every person's guide to Sukkot, Shemini Atzeret, and Simchat Torah / Ronald H. Isaacs.
      p.   cm.
   Includes bibliographical references and index.
   ISBN 0–7657–6045–2 (alk. paper)
   1. Sukkot.   2. Shemini Atzeret.   3. Simhat Torah.   I. Title.
BM695. S8I829   2000
296.4'33—dc21   98–21846
                                                                      CIP

Printed in the United States of America on acid-free paper. For information and catalog, write to Jason Aronson Inc., 230 Livingston Street, Northvale, NJ 07647-1726, or visit our website: www.aronson.com

CONTENTS

Preface ix

SUKKOT IN JEWISH HISTORY **1**
In the Bible 3
Hakhel 7
In Rabbinic Literature 8
In Post-Biblical Writings 11

SUKKOT: HOME AND SYNAGOGUE OBSERVANCE **15**
In the Home 17
In the Synagogue 31

LAWS, SYMBOLISM, AND ASSEMBLY OF THE FOUR SPECIES **43**
1 Beauty of the Four Species 50
2 Joy and the Four Species 50
3 *Mitzvah* for the Sake of Heaven 51
4 Human Body 51

5 Four Types of Jews   52
6 The Human Body and the Four Species   52
7 The Four Species and Biblical Personalities   52
8 The Four Species as the Four Kingdoms   53
9 The *Lulav* and Life   53
   Laws and Symbolism of the *Sukkah*   54

SUKKOT ODDITIES AND CURIOSITIES   **63**
 1 Season of Our Rejoicing   65
 2 Seventy Oxen   65
 3 Hebrew Letters and the Construction
    of the *Sukkah*   66
 4 The *Sukkah* and the Land of Israel   66
 5 Kissing the *Sukkah*   67
 6 The *Etrog*—A *Mitzvah* for the Sake of Heaven   67
 7 Sukkot Allusions   67
 8 "Fragrant Children"   67
 9 A Hoshanna Rabbah Women's Custom   67
10 The Torah Names for the Festival of Sukkot   68
11 Return of the Cloud of Glory   68
12 The Easy *Mitzvah* of the *Sukkah*   68
13 Exemptions Due to Distress   69
14 Yuchi Indians Observe Sukkot   69
15 The Lubavitcher *Chassidim Sukkah*mobile   69
16 Rain and Eating in a *Sukkah*   69
17 *Sukkah* of the Leviathan   70
18 A Talmudic Debate: What Is a *Sukkah?*   70
19 Hoshanna Rabbah and Your Shadow   70
20 *Etrog* Uses   70
21 Pizza in the Hut   71
22 A *Lulav* Shake   72
23 Pelted with *Etrogim*   72

SUKKOT AND SHEMINI ATZERET LEGENDS   **73**

SHEMINI ATZERET   **91**
In the Bible and the Talmud   94
In the Home   95
In the Synagogue   96

SIMCHAT TORAH   **101**
In the Home   104
In the Synagogue   104

**NOTABLE SUKKOT AND SHEMINI ATZERET
QUOTATIONS**   **111**

SUKKOT AND SIMCHAT TORAH GAMES   **119**
1 Fish   121
2 Baseball Game   123
3 Match Game   124
4 Sukkot Lotto   125
5 Word Scramble   127
6 Hot Potato   128
7 Name That Niggun   129
8 Simchat Torah Alphabet Song Game   130

SHORT STORIES   **133**
1 The *Hoshana* of Rabbi Ephraim   135
2 The Cost of an *Etrog*   140
3 How K'tonton Prayed for Rain   142
4 How K'tonton Rejoiced and Was Merry
  on Simchat Torah   147
5 Gita Meets Some Friends   151
6 The Miracle of the Myrtles   156

7 For the Sake of *Mitzvah* of the *Sukkah*   159

8 The Emir and Elijah the Prophet   161

9 The Clever Judgment   163

10 The Broken *Pitam*   165

Glossary of Terms   167

For Further Reading   171

Index   175

PREFACE

With the end of the Days of Awe and the beginning of the festival of Sukkot, the Jewish people begin the most experiential of all of the Jewish holidays. In describing the holiday of Sukkot, the Torah uses the Hebrew word *simcha* (joy) three times, more often than when mentioning any other festival. In Jewish liturgy, it is called *zeman simchatenu*—the time of rejoicing. There is a good reason for singling out Sukkot as the time of rejoicing. There is a tradition that we never sit alone in the *sukkah*. We are always joined by the *ushpizin*, the seven invited guests: Abraham, Isaac, Jacob, Joseph, David, Moses, and Aaron. This is the Jewish way of teaching that a *simcha*, a joyous occasion, can only be meaningful when celebrated with others, in a community.

Jews around the world are instructed to feel joy during the festival of Sukkot, which is a festival of thanksgiving for one's bountiful harvest. In many ways it commemorates themes similar to those of the American celebration of Thanksgiving. Some historians believe that the Pilgrims who came to America modeled their own celebration and feast after the holiday of Sukkot, known to them as Tabernacles, which they knew about from reading the Bible. The festival of Sukkot concludes with an eighth day, Shemini Atzeret, which is considered to be a separate festival and is explained in the *Midrash* as follows: "A king invited his children to a feast. After a few days, when the departure finally arrived, the king said to his children: 'I beg of you, stay another day, for it is hard to separate from you.'"

Simchat Torah, the day of rejoicing with the Torah, concludes the fall holy day season. It is filled with singing, dancing, and revelry and marks the completion of the reading of the Torah and its recommencement. Because of the laughter and gaiety, synagogue sanctuaries are generally filled to capacity with men, women, and children.

Every Person's Guide To Sukkot, Shemini Atzeret, and Simchat Torah is intended to help enhance your knowledge, observance, and creative celebration of the harvest festival season. Included is information on the historical origins of the festivals, its rituals, and its customs, both in the home and in the synagogue; a chapter on the Four Species and their symbolism; Sukkot and Simchat Torah legends; a chapter on games that can be played during the festival; curiosities and oddities; and a glossary of holiday terms.

May the days of your celebration of these holidays always be days of *simcha*—ultimate joy! And may they bring you closer to your family and to God.

SUKKOT IN JEWISH HISTORY

"You shall rejoice in your festival (Sukkot) with your son and your daughter . . . You shall hold the festival for God seven days in the place that God will choose. For God will bless all your crops and all of your undertakings, and you shall have nothing but joy" (Deuteronomy 16:14–15).

Sukkot, the fall harvest and pilgrimage festival, marks the end of the fruit harvest. It is a time of joyous celebration as we thank God for our bounty. We are also reminded of the temporary booths (*sukkot*) that sheltered the Israelites during their wanderings in the wilderness. We commemorate God's redemptive powers by living in our own booths for seven days. Sukkot thus begins the most experiential of all the Jewish holidays.

IN THE BIBLE

The holiday of Sukkot, called *hechag* ("the festival par excellence") in the Bible (Leviticus 23:39–40), celebrates both history and nature. It begins on the fifteenth of the Hebrew month of Tishri and commemorates the booths in which the children of Israel dwelt in the wilderness after the Exodus from Egypt: "The people shall dwell in booths for seven days, so that your generations may know that I made the children of Israel to dwell in booths, when I brought them out of the land of Egypt" (Leviticus 23:39–43).

In Exodus 23:16 the Bible refers to "the feast of ingathering at the end of the year, when you gather in your labors out of your field." In Deuteronomy 16:13, the festival is described thusly: "You shall keep the feast of tabernacles seven days, after that you have gathered in from your threshing floor and from your winepress."

Since ancient times Sukkot was one of the most important feasts of the Israelites and was therefore called "the feast of the Lord" (Leviticus 23:29; Judges 21:19) or simply "the feast" (1 Kings 8:2, 65).

Another biblical commandment associated with the festival of Sukkot is that of the four varieties of trees that the children of Israel were enjoined to take with which to rejoice with God: ". . . you shall take the fruit of goodly trees, branches of palm trees, boughs of leafy trees and willows of the brook, and you shall rejoice before the Lord your God seven days" (Leviticus 23:40).

The dedication of the Temple in Jerusalem during the reign of King Solomon took place on Sukkot. This historic event is detailed in the First Book of Kings: 8:2–6:

All the men of Israel assembled themselves unto King Solomon at the feast, in the month of Etanim, which is the seventh month. And all the elders came, and the priests took up the Ark. And they brought up the Ark of God, and the tent of meetings, and all the holy vessels that were in the Tent. And King Solomon and the congregation of Israel, that were assembled unto him, were with him before the Ark, sacrificing sheep and oxen . . . And the priests brought in the Ark of the covenant of God to its place, into the sanctuary of the house, to the most holy place, even under the wings of cherubim.

First Kings also describes the rebellion of Jeroboam against Rehoboam, the successor of King Solomon. To show his independence, Jeroboam moved the date for the commemoration of the festival of Sukkot:

Then Jeroboam built Shechem in the hill country of Ephraim, and dwelt therein. And he went out from there and built Penuel. And Jeroboam said in his heart: "Now will the kingdom return to the house of David. If this people go up to offer sacrifices in the house of the Lord at Jerusalem, then will the heart of this people turn back to their lord, even unto Rehoboam king of Judah. And they will kill me, and return to Rehoboam king of Judah."

And Jeroboam ordained a feast in the eighth month, on the fifteenth day of the month, like unto the feast that was in Judah . . . And he went up to the altar which he had made in Beth El on the fifteenth day in the eighth month, even in the month which he had devised of his own heart; and he ordained a feast for the children of Israel, and went up to the altar to offer. (1 Kings 12:25–27, 32–33)

The Book of Ezra also contains an account of the reinstitution of the celebration of Sukkot in Jerusalem (sixth century B.C.E.) after the Babylonian exile:

And when the seventh month was come, and the children of Israel were in the cities, the people gathered themselves together as one man to Jerusalem. Then stood up Jeshua the son of Jozadak, and his brothers the priests, and Zerubbabel the son of Shealtiel, and his brothers, and built the altar of the God of Israel, to offer burnt offerings thereon, as it is written in the law of Moses, the man of God. And they set the altar upon its bases; for fear was upon them because of the people of the countries, and they offered burnt offerings thereon to God, even burnt offerings morning and evening. And they kept the feast of tabernacles, as it is written, and offered the daily burnt offerings by number, according to the ordinance, as the duty of every day required. (Ezra 3:1–5)

The prophet Zechariah envisioned a time when all the nations of the world would worship one God and observe the festival of Sukkot:

And it shall come to pass, that every one that is left of all the nations that came against Jerusalem shall go up from year to year to worship the Sovereign, God of hosts, and to keep the feast of tabernacles. And it shall be, that whoso of the families of the earth goes not to Jerusalem to worship the Sovereign, God of hosts, upon them there shall be no rain. And if the family of Egypt does not go up, and does not come, they shall have no overflow. There shall be the plague, wherewith God will smite the

nations that do not go up to keep the feast of tabernacles. This shall be the punishment of Egypt, and the
punishment of all the nations that do not go up to keep
the feast of tabernacles.

HAKHEL

A most interesting biblical ceremony is that called *hakhel*
("assembly"): "At the end of every seven years, at the
time of the year of release, at the Festival of Sukkot,"
there is to take place an assembly of the whole people,
"men, women, children and the stranger that is within
your gates." The purpose of the assembly is "that they
may hear and so learn to revere God and to observe
faithfully every word of this teaching" (Deuteronomy
31:10–13). According to rabbinic interpretation (Talmud,
Sotah 7:8), such was the instruction that Moses gave to
Joshua when he commanded him to assemble young
and old on Sukkot at the end of the Sabbatical year and
to read before them sections from the Book of Deuteronomy. This occasion, which must have constituted a
veritable people's festival, was intended to emphasize, in
particular, the nation's faith in God and in God's Torah.

In later years, the duty of reading sections from the
Torah devolved upon the King, who received the Torah
standing and read it sitting. We are not told in the Bible
on what day of Sukkot the *hakhel* celebrations took
place, but Maimonides, the medieval commentator, suggests that it was on the second day.

After the destruction of the Temple, when Israel went
into exile, *hakhel* was discontinued, for it can be ob-

served only when Israel dwells securely in its land. With
the beginning of Israel's ingathering in its ancient home-
land and the re-establishment of the State of Israel, the
Chief Rabbinate of Israel decided to reintroduce a symbolic form of the *hakhel* ceremony.

IN RABBINIC LITERATURE

As mentioned previously, two special observances are
described in the Book of Leviticus (23:39–43): that the
people should dwell in booths for seven days, so "that
your generations may know that I made the children of
Israel to dwell in booths, when I brought them out of the
land of Egypt," and that the people were to take on the
first day "the fruit of goodly trees, branches of palm
trees, and boughs of thick trees and willows of the
brook" to "rejoice before God." Rabbinic authorities
named these the *arba'ah minim*, the four species. The
fruits of goodly trees is the citron (*etrog* in Hebrew), the
boughs of thick trees are the myrtle twigs (*hadasim*, in
Hebrew), the palm branch is the *lulav*, and the willows
are the *aravot*. In the Book of Nehemiah it is said that
from the days of Joshua to Nehemiah, the people had
not dwelt in booths (Nehemiah 8:17), but in the same
chapter it is stated: "Go forth to the mount, and fetch
olive branches, and branches of wild olive, and myrtle
branches, and palm branches, and branches of thick
trees, to make booths as it is written" (Nehemiah 8:15).
There is no mention of olive branches in Leviticus and
none of willows in Nehemiah. Moreover, from Nehemiah it would appear that the various plants were

used to cover the booths, whereas in rabbinic tradition, the command to dwell in booths and the command to take the four species are treated as two separate precepts. In Zechariah's vision all the nations of the world will come to Jerusalem in the new age to celebrate the festival of Sukkot (Zechariah 14:16).

According to the rabbis, biblical law obliges every male to take the four species in the hand on the first day of Sukkot. The rabbis, however, understood the reference in the verse "to rejoice before the Lord your God seven days" to apply to the Temple, where the four species had to be taken each day. After the destruction of the Temple, Jochanan ben Zakkai ordained that wherever Jews celebrate Sukkot, the four species should be taken in the hand for seven days in commemoration of the Temple (Talmud, *Sukkah* 3:12).

The four species were to be held in the hand while the *Hallel* Psalms of praise (Psalms 113–118) are chanted and they were to be waved at the beginning of Psalms 118 and while reciting verse 25 of the psalm (Talmud, *Sukkah* 3:4). The *lulav* was to be held in the right hand together with three *hadasim* and two *aravot* and the *etrog* in the left hand (Talmud, *Sukkah* 3:4). The *lulav*, the largest of the four species, gives its name to the four so that the blessing is: Praised are You Who has sanctified us with His commandments and commanded us to take the *lulav* (Talmud, *Sukkah* 46a).

Interestingly, rabbinic authorities mention a special ceremony of "water libation" during the seven days of Sukkot (Talmud, *Sukkah* 4:9). The special rites of water libation, accompanied by the playing of the flute, took place only on *chol ha-moed* (intermediate day) and not

on the holy day itself. The ceremony was known as
simchat bet ha-sho'evah ("the rejoicing of the place of
water drawing"), based evidently on Isaiah 12:3: "Therefore, with joy shall you draw water out of the wells of
salvation" (Talmud, *Sukkah* 5:1). There were said to be
three gigantic golden candlesticks in the Temple court
that were lit on these occasions, and there was not a
courtyard in Jerusalem that did not reflect the light of the
bet ha-sho'evah (Talmud, *Sukkah* 5:2–3).

Here is the Talmud's own description of the water
libation ceremony:

> Men of piety and good works used to dance before them
> with burning torches in their hands, singing songs and
> praises. Levites without number with harps, lyres, cym-
> bals, and trumpets and other musical instruments were
> there upon the fifteen steps leading down from the court
> of the Israelites to the court of the women, correspond-
> ing to the fifteen songs of ascents in their Psalms. It was
> upon these that the Levites stood with their instruments
> of music and sang their songs. Two *kohanim* stood by
> the upper gate which led down from the court of the
> Israelites to the court of the women, with two instru-
> ments in their hands. When the cock crowed they
> sounded a *tekiah*, a *teruah*, and again a *tekiah*. When
> they reached the tenth step they sounded a *tekiah*, a
> *teruah*, and again a *tekiah*. When they reached the court
> they sounded a *tekiah*, a *teruah*, and a *tekiah*. They
> proceeded to sound their instruments, until they reached
> the gate which led out at the east; they turned their faces
> from east to west and proclaimed: "Our Fathers who
> were in this place stood with their backs toward the
> Temple of the Lord and their faces toward the west, and

they worshiped the sun toward the east, but as for us, our eyes are turned to the Lord." Rabbi Judah stated, They used to repeat the last words and say, "We are the Lord's and our eyes are turned to the Lord." (Talmud, *Sukkah* 5:1–4)

IN POST-BIBLICAL WRITINGS

The books of the Apocrypha, representing a substantial ethical literature, reflect the developments of social and religious life among the Jewish people during the period of the Second Temple. Since they were not included in the Hebrew Bible, the Talmud refers to them as *sefarim chitzonim*, "outside books." Otherwise, they are called "apocrypha" (hidden away) or "pseudepigrapha" (denoting books ascribed to imaginary authors who take pen names from the great heroes of Israel's history).

The Second Book of Maccabees is filled with stories of defiant martyrdom during the Maccabean uprising. Its writing is ascribed to Jason of Cyrene, a Hellenistic Jew, and presents allusions to the observance of Sukkot as coinciding with that of Hanukkah:

Maccabeus with his men, led by the Lord, recovered the Temple and the city of Jerusalem. He demolished the altars erected by the heathens in the public square and their sacred precincts as well. When they had purified the sanctuary, they constructed another altar, then striking fire from flints, they offered the lights, and the shew bread . . . The sanctuary was purified on the twenty-fifth day of Kislev . . . This joyful celebration went on for eight days. It was like Sukkot, for they recalled how only a short time before they had kept the festival while living like animals in the mountains, and so they carried *lulavim* and *etrogim* and they chanted hymns to God Who triumphantly led them to the purification of the Temple. A measure was passed by the public assembly that the entire Jewish people should observe these days every year. (2 Maccabees 10:1–8)

From this text we are presented with the amazing fact that Hanukkah began as a second celebration of the eight-day Sukkot holiday, since during the war it was impossible to properly celebrate Sukkot in its proper season.

The pseudepigraphical Book of Jubilees consists of a history of humankind related by an angel to Moses on Mount Sinai with specifications of the jubilee of each event. The author assumes the Torah to have been current from the earliest human period but forgotten until Moses was reminded of it. The Book of Jubilees ascribes the origin of the festival of Sukkot to the patriarch Abraham:

We the angels announced to Abraham all the things which had been decreed concerning him, and we announced to Sarah all that we had told him, and they both rejoiced with exceeding great joy. And he built there an altar to God Who had delivered him, and Who was making him rejoice in the land of his sojourning, and he celebrated a festival of joy in this month seven days, near the altar he had built at the Well of the Oath. And he built booths for himself and for his servants on this festival, and he was the first to celebrate the Feast of Tabernacles on the earth. And he celebrated this feast during seven days, rejoicing with all his heart and with all his soul. (Book of Jubilees 16:16, 19–21)

In the Book of Jubilees another reference to Sukkot presents the patriarch Jacob adding an eighth day to the festival:

On the fifteenth of this month, Jacob brought to the altar fourteen oxen from among the cattle, and twenty-eight rams, forty-nine sheep, and seven lambs, and twenty-one kids of the goats as a burnt offering on the altar of sacrifice, well-pleasing for a sweet savor before God. This was his offering, in consequence of the vow which he had vowed that he would give a tenth . . . and thus he did for seven days. And he and all his sons and his men were eating this with joy there seven days and blessing and thanking the Lord who had delivered him out of all his tribulation and had given him his vow . . . And he celebrated there yet another day, and he sacrificed thereon according to all that he sacrificed on the former days, and called its name "addition," for this day was added and the former days he called "the feast." (Book of Jubilees 32:4–7, 27)

The historian Flavius Josephus wrote the following in his *Antiquities of the Jews*, relating to the festival of Sukkot as a turning point to the winter season:

On the fifteenth of this same month (Sukkot), at which the turning point to the winter season is now reached, Moses bids each family to fix up tents, apprehensive of the cold as a protection against the year's inclemency. Moreover, when they should have won their fatherland,

they were to repair to that city which they would in
honor of the Temple regard as their metropolis, and
there for eight days keep the festival. They were to offer
burnt offerings and sacrifices of thanksgiving to God in
those days, bearing in their hands a bouquet composed
of myrtle and willow with a branch of palm, along with
fruit of the *etrog*. On the first of those days their burnt
sacrifice should consist of thirteen oxen, as many lambs
and one over, two rams, and a kid to boot in propiation
for sins. On the following days the same number of
lambs and of rams is sacrificed, together with the kid, but
they reduce that of the oxen by one daily until they reach
seven. They abstain from all work on the eighth day and,
as we have said, sacrifice to God a calf, a ram, seven
lambs, and a kid in propiation for sins. Such are the rites,
handed down from their forefathers, which the Hebrews
observe when they erect their tabernacles. (*Antiquities
of the Jews* 3.10.45)

Sukkot: Home and Synagogue Observance

IN THE HOME

Preparation for the Festival of Sukkot

The four days between Yom Kippur and Sukkot are festive in Jewish tradition, because they are the anniversary of the fourteen-day dedication of the Holy Temple by King Solomon. Fasting is prohibited, including even an individual fast on a parent's *yahrzeit*.

Preparation for the festival of Sukkot includes the building of the *sukkah* and the purchasing of an *etrog* and the other species that accompany it.

There is an ancient maxim: "If an opportunity to perform a *mitzvah* presents itself to you, do not be slow in performing it" (*Mechilta*, Tractate *d'Pisha, parasha* 9). Hence, according to the Code of Jewish law, the custom is to begin the building of the *sukkah* immediately after Yom Kippur. Some pious Jews drive in the first nail, so to speak, the night after Yom Kippur so as to proceed directly from one *mitzvah* to another.

The most important religious obligation of Sukkot is dwelling in the *sukkah*. The *sukkah* is a temporary structure constructed for the festival of Sukkot. Its impermanence is to remind us of the portability of the huts in the wilderness during the wandering of the Israelites for forty years. It must be erected in the open air, under the sky, not in a room or under a tree. Its height must not exceed thirty feet, because it would then cease to be a temporary dwelling since the walls would have to be exceedingly strong. It consists of four walls and a covering called *sechach*, which is material that grows from the soil. The covering is usually tree branches and often bamboo and is placed on the roof so that it is loose enough that one can see the sky, yet thick enough so that the shadow it casts on the ground exceeds the light thrown by the sun.

The walls of the *sukkah* may be constructed of any material and ought to be strong enough to withstand the impact of ordinary winds.

On the basis of the rabbinic maxim that the commandments should have aesthetic appeal (Talmud, *Shabbat* 133b), it has become customary to decorate the *sukkah*. Much creative effort goes into the decorating of the *sukkah*. The Talmud (*Betzah* 30b) suggests hanging handmade carpets and tapestries, nuts, pomegranates, branches of grapevine, and wreaths of ears of corn. Today paper chains, Rosh Hashanah (New Year's) greeting cards, Indian corn, gourds, colored lights, and Jewish pictures of scenes of Israel are popular adornments to the *sukkah*.

Today the *sukkah* is used mostly for eating, although there are still people who will opt (weather permitting) to sleep in their *sukkah*.

Before the advent of the festival, the custom is for each family to provide itself with the so-called four species, also called the *lulav* and *etrog* (palm branch with willow and myrtle leaves and the citron).

The biblical source for this commandment is the verse in Leviticus 23:40: "On the first day you shall take the product of hadar trees, branches of palm trees, boughs of leafy trees, and willows of the brook." The willow and the palm branch are mentioned explicitly. The Talmud (*Sukkah* 35a) explains that "the product of hadar trees" refers to the *etrog* and that "boughs of leafy trees" refers to the myrtle (Talmud, *Sukkah* 35a). While the *etrog* retained its name, the other three species are together called the *lulav* because of the prominence of the palm branch.

The *lulav* should have one palm branch, two willow and three myrtle twigs. They are tied together in the direction in which they grow, the myrtle on the right of the palm branch and the willow on the left, with the spine of the palm branch facing the holder.

Pious people go to great lengths to acquire an *etrog* and a *lulav* that are particularly pleasing to the eye. Here, shape and color are important factors. The traditional recommendation is that the *etrog* should taper upward at the top rather than be spherical. The surface should not be smooth like a lemon but rather rough and ridged. There should be no blotches or discolorations on the skin and it should be yellow in color.

The *lulav* should be fresh and its leaves should not spread out nor should the tip be broken off. The myrtle and willow leaves should be green, fresh, and with the leaves intact.

Customs and Rituals in the *Sukkah*

On the first night of Sukkot, we light candles in the *sukkah* and recite: "Praised are You, Adonai our God, Ruler of the universe, Who has made us holy by *mitzvot* and commanded us to kindle the festival lights." Then we recite the *shehecheyanu* blessing: "Praised are You, Adonai our God, Ruler of the universe, for keeping us in life, sustaining us and for helping us to reach this festive day." The festival *Kiddush* over the wine is recited, followed by the special blessing in which we praise God for commanding us to dwell in a *sukkah*: "Praised are You, Adonai our God, Ruler of the universe, Who has sanctified us through His commandments and instructed us to dwell in the *sukkah*."

Following this special blessing comes the blessing that accompanies the ritual washing of the hands and the blessing over the bread. During the meal, many families enjoy singing festive songs. The meal concludes with the recitation of the blessing after the meal.

Basic Blessings

Following are the basic blessings recited in the *sukkah* during the festival of Sukkot.

BASIC BLESSINGS

Candlelighting

בָּרוּךְ אַתָּה יהוה אֱלֹהֵינוּ מֶלֶךְ הָעוֹלָם, אֲשֶׁר קִדְּשָׁנוּ בְּמִצְוֹתָיו
וְצִוָּנוּ לְהַדְלִיק נֵר שֶׁל (שַׁבָּת וְשֶׁל) יוֹם טוֹב.

*Barukh atah adonai eloheinu melekh ha'olam asher
kid'shanu b'mitzvotav v'tzivanu l'hadlik neir shel (shabbat
v'shel) yom tov.*

Praised are You, Adonai our God, Sovereign of the
Universe, who has made us holy by giving us
commandments and commanded us to light the (Shabbat
and) festival candles.

On Dwelling in the Sukkah

בָּרוּךְ אַתָּה יהוה אֱלֹהֵינוּ מֶלֶךְ הָעוֹלָם, אֲשֶׁר קִדְּשָׁנוּ בְּמִצְוֹתָיו
וְצִוָּנוּ לֵישֵׁב בַּסֻּכָּה.

*Barukh atah adonai eloheinu melekh ha'olam asher
kid'shanu b'mitzvotav v'tzivanu leisheiv basukkah.*

Praised are You, Adonai our God, Sovereign of the
Universe, who has made us holy by mitzvot and instructed
us to dwell in the sukkah.

Shehecheyanu Prayer for the Gift of Life
(first day only)

בָּרוּךְ אַתָּה יהוה אֱלֹהֵינוּ מֶלֶךְ הָעוֹלָם, שֶׁהֶחֱיָנוּ וְקִיְּמָנוּ וְהִגִּיעָנוּ
לַזְּמַן הַזֶּה.

*Barukh atah adonai eloheinu melekh ha'olam
shehecheyanu v'kiymanu v'higi'anu laz'man hazeh.*

Praised are You, Adonai our God, Sovereign of the
Universe, who has kept us in life, sustained us, and enabled
us to reach this festive time.

Festival Kiddush

בָּרוּךְ אַתָּה יהוה אֱלֹהֵינוּ מֶלֶךְ הָעוֹלָם, בּוֹרֵא פְּרִי הַגָּפֶן.
בָּרוּךְ אַתָּה יהוה אֱלֹהֵינוּ מֶלֶךְ הָעוֹלָם, אֲשֶׁר בָּחַר בָּנוּ מִכָּל־עָם
וְרוֹמְמָנוּ מִכָּל־לָשׁוֹן, וְקִדְּשָׁנוּ בְּמִצְוֹתָיו. וַתִּתֶּן לָנוּ יהוה אֱלֹהֵינוּ
בְּאַהֲבָה (שַׁבָּתוֹת לִמְנוּחָה וּ)מוֹעֲדִים לְשִׂמְחָה, חַגִּים וּזְמַנִּים לְשָׂשׂוֹן,
אֶת־יוֹם (הַשַּׁבָּת הַזֶּה וְאֶת־יוֹם) חַג הַסֻּכּוֹת הַזֶּה, זְמַן שִׂמְחָתֵנוּ,
(בְּאַהֲבָה) מִקְרָא קֹדֶשׁ, זֵכֶר לִיצִיאַת מִצְרָיִם. כִּי־בָנוּ בָחַרְתָּ וְאוֹתָנוּ
קִדַּשְׁתָּ מִכָּל־הָעַמִּים, (וְשַׁבָּת) וּמוֹעֲדֵי קָדְשֶׁךָ (בְּאַהֲבָה וּבְרָצוֹן)
בְּשִׂמְחָה וּבְשָׂשׂוֹן הִנְחַלְתָּנוּ. בָּרוּךְ אַתָּה יְיָ, מְקַדֵּשׁ (הַשַּׁבָּת וְ)
יִשְׂרָאֵל וְהַזְּמַנִּים.

*Barukh atah adonai eloheinu melekh ha'olam, borei p'ri
hagafen. Barukh atah adonai eloheinu melekh ha'olam,
asher bachar banu mikol am v'ro-m'manu mekol lashon
v'kid'shanu b'mitzvotav vatiten lanu adonai eloheinu b'ahavah (shabbatot lim'nuchah u) mo'adim l'simchah chagim
uz'manim l'sasson et yom (hashabbat hazeh v'et yom)
chag hasukkot hazeh, z'man simchateinu (b'ahavah) mikra
kodesh zeikher litzi'at mitzrayim. Ki vanu vacharta v'otanu
kidashta mikol ha'amim (v'shabbat) umo'adei kodsh'kha
(b'ahavah uv'ratzon) b'simchah uv'sasson hinchaltanu.
Barukh atah adonai, m'kadesh (hashabbat v') yisra'eil
v'haz'manim.*

Praised are You, Eternal our God, Sovereign of the Universe
who creates fruit of the vine.

Praised are You, Eternal our God, Sovereign of the Universe who has chosen and distinguished us from among all others by adding holiness to our lives with mitzvot. Lovingly have You given us (Shabbat for rest,) festivals for joy and holidays for happiness, among them this (Shabbat and this) day of Sukkot, season of our joy, a day of sacred assembly recalling the Exodus from Egypt. Thus You have chosen us, endowing us with holiness from among all peoples by granting us (Shabbat and) Your hallowed festivals (lovingly and gladly) in happiness and joy. Praised are You, God who hallows (Shabbat and) the people Israel and the festivals.

Blessing for Washing Hands

בָּרוּךְ אַתָּה יהוה אֱלֹהֵינוּ מֶלֶךְ הָעוֹלָם, אֲשֶׁר קִדְּשָׁנוּ בְּמִצְוֹתָיו וְצִוָּנוּ עַל נְטִילַת יָדָיִם.

Barukh atah adonai eloheinu melekh ha'olam asher kid'shanu b'mitzvotav v'tzivanu al n'tilat yadayim.

Praised are You, Adonai, Sovereign of the Universe, who has made us holy by mitzvot and instructed us to wash our hands.

Blessing over Bread

בָּרוּךְ אַתָּה יהוה אֱלֹהֵינוּ מֶלֶךְ הָעוֹלָם, הַמּוֹצִיא לֶחֶם מִן הָאָרֶץ.

Barukh atah adonai eloheinu melekh ha'olam hamotzi lechem min ha'aretz.

Praised are You, Adonai our God, Sovereign of the Universe, who brings forth bread from the earth.

Birkat Hamazon (Blessing After the Meal)

רַבּוֹתַי נְבָרֵךְ.

Rabotai n'vareikh

Friends, let us give thanks.

The others respond, and the leader repeats:

יְהִי שֵׁם יְיָ מְבֹרָךְ מֵעַתָּה וְעַד עוֹלָם.

Y'hi sheim adonai m'vorakh mei'atah v'ad olam.

May God be praised now and forever.

The leader continues:

בִּרְשׁוּת רַבּוֹתַי, נְבָרֵךְ (אֱלֹהֵינוּ) שֶׁאָכַלְנוּ מִשֶּׁלוֹ.

Bir'shut rabotai n'vareikh (eloheinu) she'akhalnu mishelo.

With your consent friends, let us praise (our God) the One of whose food we have partaken.

The others respond, and the leader repeats:

בָּרוּךְ (אֱלֹהֵינוּ) שֶׁאָכַלְנוּ מִשֶּׁלוֹ וּבטוּבוֹ חָיִינוּ.

Barukh (eloheinu) she'akhalnu mishelo uv'tuvo chayinu.

Praised be (our God) the One whose food we have partaken and by whose goodness we live.

Leader and others:

בָּרוּךְ הוּא וּבָרוּךְ שְׁמוֹ.

Barukh hu uvarukh sh'mo.

Praised be God and praised be God's name.

בָּרוּךְ אַתָּה יהוה אֱלֹהֵינוּ מֶלֶךְ הָעוֹלָם,הַזָּן אֶת־הָעוֹלָם כֻּלּוֹ בְּטוּבוֹ,
בְּחֵן בְּחֶסֶד וּבְרַחֲמִים. הוּא נוֹתֵן לֶחֶם לְכָל־בָּשָׂר כִּי לְעוֹלָם חַסְדּוֹ.
וּבְטוּבוֹ הַגָּדוֹל תָּמִיד לֹא חָסַר לָנוּ וְאַל יֶחְסַר לָנוּ מָזוֹן לְעוֹלָם
וָעֶד בַּעֲבוּר שְׁמוֹ הַגָּדוֹל, כִּי הוּא אֵל זָן וּמְפַרְנֵס לַכֹּל וּמֵטִיב לַכֹּל
וּמֵכִין מָזוֹן לְכָל־בְּרִיּוֹתָיו אֲשֶׁר בָּרָא. בָּרוּךְ אַתָּה יו ׃וה, הַזָּן אֶת־הַכֹּל.

*Barukh atah adonai, eloheinu melekh ha'olam, hazan et
ha'olam kulo b'tuvo b'chein, b'chesed, uv'rachamim. Hu
notein lechem l'khol basar, ki l'olam chasdo. Uv'tuvo hagadol, tamid lo chasar lanu, v'al yechsar lanu mazon l'olam
va'ed ba'avur sh'mo hagadol, ki hu el zan um'farneis lakol,
umeitiv lakol, umeikhin mazon l'khol b'riyotav asher bara.
Barukh atah adonai, hazan et hakol.*

Praised are You, Eternal, our God, Sovereign of the Universe who sustains the whole world with kindness and
compassion. You provide food for every creature, for
Your love endures forever. Your great goodness has never
failed us. Your great glory assures us nourishment. All life
is God's creation and God is good to all, providing every
creature with food and sustenance. Praised are You, God
who sustains all life.

נוֹדֶה לְךָ יְיָ אֱלֹהֵינוּ עַל שֶׁהִנְחַלְתָּ לַאֲבוֹתֵינוּ אֶרֶץ חֶמְדָּה טוֹבָה
וּרְחָבָה, בְּרִית וְתוֹרָה, חַיִּים וּמָזוֹן. יִתְבָּרַךְ שִׁמְךָ בְּפִי כָּל־חַי תָּמִיד
לְעוֹלָם וָעֶד. כַּכָּתוּב: וְאָכַלְתָּ וְשָׂבַעְתָּ וּבֵרַכְתָּ אֶת־יְיָ אֱלֹהֶיךָ עַל
הָאָרֶץ הַטּוֹבָה אֲשֶׁר נָתַן לָךְ. בָּרוּךְ אַתָּה יְיָ, עַל הָאָרֶץ וְעַל
הַמָּזוֹן.

*Nodeh l'kha adonai eloheinu al shehinchalta la'avoteinu
eretz chemdah, tovah ur'chavah, b'rit v'torah, chayim um-
azon. Yitbarakh shimkha b'fi khol chai tamid l'olam va'ed.
Kakatuv v'akhalta v'savata uveirakhta et adonai elohekha
al ha'aretz hatovah asher natan lakh. Barukh atah adonai,
al ha'aretz v'al hamazon.*

We thank you, God, for the pleasing, ample, desirable
land which You gave to our ancestors, for the covenant
and Torah, for life and sustenance. May You forever be
praised by all who live, as it is written in the Torah:
"When you have eaten and are satisfied, you shall praise
the Eternal your God for the good land which God has
given you." Praised are You, God, for the land and for
sustenance.

וּבְנֵה יְרוּשָׁלַיִם עִיר הַקֹּדֶשׁ בִּמְהֵרָה בְיָמֵנוּ. בָּרוּךְ אַתָּה יְיָ, בּוֹנֵה
בְּרַחֲמָיו יְרוּשָׁלָיִם. אָמֵן.

*Uv'neih yerushalayim ir hakodesh bimheirah v'yameinu.
Barukh atah adonai, boneh v'rachamav yerushalayim.
Amen.*

Fully rebuild Jerusalem, the holy city, soon in our time.
Praised are You, Adonai, who in mercy rebuilds Jerusalem.
Amen.

בָּרוּךְ אַתָּה יהוה אֱלֹהֵינוּ מֶלֶךְ הָעוֹלָם, הַמֶּלֶךְ הַטּוֹב וְהַמֵּטִיב
לַכֹּל. הוּא הֵטִיב, הוּא מֵטִיב, הוּא יֵיטִיב לָנוּ. הוּא גְמָלָנוּ הוּא
גוֹמְלֵנוּ הוּא יִגְמְלֵנוּ לָעַד חֵן וָחֶסֶד וְרַחֲמִים וִיזַכֵּנוּ לִימוֹת הַמָּשִׁיחַ.

*Barukh atah adonai, eloheinu melekh ha'olam, hamelekh
hatov v'hameitiv lakol. Hu heitiv, hu meitiv, hu yeitiv
lanu. Hu g'malanu, hu gomleinu, hu yigm'leinu la'ad chein
vachesed v'rachamim, vizakeinu limot hamashi'ach.*

Praised are You, God, Sovereign of the Universe who is
good to all, whose goodness is constant through all time.
Favor us with kindness and compassion now and in the
future as in the past. May we be worthy of the days of
the Messiah.

[On Shabbat add:

הָרַחֲמָן, הוּא יַנְחִילֵנוּ יוֹם שֶׁכֻּלּוֹ שַׁבָּת וּמְנוּחָה לְחַיֵּי הָעוֹלָמִים.

*Harachaman hu yanchileinu yom shekulo shabbat umenu-
chah l'chayei ha'olamim.*

May the Merciful grant us a day of true shabbat rest,
reflecting the life of eternity.]

[On festivals:

הָרַחֲמָן, הוּא יַנְחִילֵנוּ יוֹם שֶׁכֻּלּוֹ טוֹב

Harachaman hu yanchileinu yom shekulo tov.

May the Merciful grant us a day filled with the spirit of
the festival.]

וְנִשָׂא בְרָכָה מֵאֵת יְיָ וּצְדָקָה מֵאֱלֹהֵי יִשְׁעֵנוּ וְנִמְצָא חֵן וְשֵׂכֶל טוֹב
בְּעֵינֵי אֱלֹהִים וְאָדָם. עֹשֶׂה שָׁלוֹם בִּמְרוֹמָיו הוּא יַעֲשֶׂה שָׁלוֹם
עָלֵינוּ וְעַל כָּל־יִשְׂרָאֵל, וְאִמְרוּ אָמֵן.

*V'nisa v'rakhah mei'eit adonai utz'dakah mei'elohei
yish'einu. V'nimtza chein v'seikhel tov b'einei elohim
v'adam. Oseh shalom bimromav hu ya'aseh shalom aleinu
v'al kol yisra'eil. V'imru amen.*

May we receive blessings from God, loving-kindness from
the God of our deliverance. May we find grace and good
favor before God and all people. May God who brings
peace to the universe bring peace to us and to all the
people Israel. And let us say: Amen.

Ushpizin

On Sukkot there is a beautiful custom of inviting *ushpizin*, symbolic guests, each day to join us in the *sukkah*.
These honorary biblical guests are Abraham, Isaac,
Jacob, Joseph, Moses, Aaron, and David. One is invited
each day. The custom of *ushpizin* rests on a kabbalistic
(mystical) statement to the effect that the Divine Glory
shelters the *sukkah* beneath its wings, and Abraham, in
the company of six righteous men, enters to participate
in the hospitality of the Jew who properly observes the
precept of the *sukkah*.

Recent *ushpizin* customs include the invitation to

Jewish matriarchs (Sarah, Rebekah, Rachel, and Leah) and other important Jewish biblical women, including Miriam, Esther, and Deborah. Sephardic Jews set aside an elaborately decorated chair for the honored guest and recite, "This is the chair of the *ushpizin*." Some families today choose to make a list of their contemporary heroes, and each night have a different family member invite a new imaginary guest into the *sukkah*. This activity can be enhanced by having a family member role-play a contemporary guest. Family members are asked to guess the identity of the contemporary guest, and this can prove to be quite entertaining.

In the literature of the *Kabbalah* the *ushpizin* are known as "exalted holy guests." The following citation from the mystical Book of the *Zohar* describes the *ushpizin* custom:

> When a man sits in the *sukkah* of the shadow of faith, the Divine Glory spreads its wings over him from above, and Abraham and five righteous ones and David with them make their abode with him. A man should rejoice each day of the festival with these guests who abide with him . . . Accordingly, when Rav Hamnuna the Elder would enter the *sukkah* he used to stand inside the door and say, "Let us invite the guests and prepare a table." And he used to stand up and greet them, saying, "In booths you shall dwell seven days. Sit, most exalted guests, sit. Sit, guests of faith, sit." He would then raise hands in joy and say, "Happy is our portion; happy is the portion of Israel . . ."

One must also gladden the poor, because the portion of these guests whom he invites must go to the poor. For

if a man sits in the shadow of faith and invites those
guests and does not give them their portion, they all hold
aloof from him. (*Zohar, Emor* 103a)

Thus, according to the *Zohar*, one should rejoice
together with an equal number of needy people sharing
one's meals in the *sukkah*.

Following is a traditional suggested text for the ceremony of the *ushpizin*:

Behold I am prepared and ready to perform the commandment of the *sukkah* as God has commanded me: In
sukkot you shall dwell for seven days in order that your
generation may know that I caused the children of Israel
to dwell in *sukkot* when I brought them out of the land
of Egypt.

Be seated, be seated, exalted guests. Be seated, guests
of faithfulness; be seated in the shade of the Holy
Blessed One. May the pleasantness of my God be upon
us. May God establish our handiwork for us.

Each day: I invite to my meal the exalted guests:
Abraham Isaac, Jacob, Joseph, Moses, Aaron, and David.

On the first day: May it please you, Abraham, my
exalted guest, that all the other exalted guests dwell here
with me and you—Isaac, Jacob, Joseph, Moses, Aaron,
and David.

On the second day: May it please you, Isaac, my
exalted guest, that all the other exalted guests dwell here
with me and with you—Abraham, Jacob, Joseph, Moses,
Aaron, and David.

On the third day: May it please you, Jacob, my
exalted guest, that all the other exalted guests dwell here
with me and with you—Abraham, Isaac, Joseph, Moses,
Aaron, and David.

On the fourth day: May it please you, Joseph, my exalted guest, that all the other exalted guests dwell here with me and with you—Abraham, Isaac, Jacob, Moses, Aaron, and David.

On the fifth day: May it please you, Moses, my exalted guest, that all the other exalted guests dwell here with me and with you—Abraham, Isaac, Jacob, Joseph, Aaron, and David.

On the sixth day: May it please you, Aaron, my exalted guest, that all the other exalted guests dwell here with me and with you—Abraham, Isaac, Jacob, Joseph, Moses, and David.

On Hoshanna Rabbah: May it please you, David, my exalted guest, that all the other exalted guests dwell here with me and with you—Abraham, Isaac, Jacob, Joseph, Moses, and Aaron.

IN THE SYNAGOGUE

Synagogue services on the first two days of Sukkot include the recitation of the *Hallel* Psalms of Praise. Before the beginning of the *Hallel* service, the blessing over the *lulav* and the *etrog* is recited. The *lulav* is taken in the right hand and the *etrog* in the left hand, held together in the position in which they grow (i.e, tip upward). Since a benediction must precede the performance of a commandment, we begin by holding the *etrog* in the reverse position (i.e., with its tip [called the *pitam*] downward and stem [called the *oketz*] upward) and the following two blessings are recited: "Praised are You, Adonai our God, Ruler of the universe, Who has made us holy by *mitzvot* and Who gave us the *mitzvah* to take up the *lulav*."

Each year, the following is recited upon taking the *lulav* for the first time: "Praised are You, Adonai our God, Ruler of the universe, Who has kept us in life and sustained us, enabling us to reach this day."

The *etrog* is then reversed so that it is held in the position of its growth and, together with the *lulav*, both are shaken three times in each direction, successively, in the following order: pointing ahead of you, to your right side, behind you over your right shoulder, to your left side, and then, while held in front of you, raised up and lowered.

The waving of the *lulav* and *etrog* is also done each time the verse *Hodu l'Adonai kee tov kee l'olam chasdo*—"Acclaim God for God is good, and God's love endures forever" (Psalms 118:1). Since the verse has six Hebrew words (apart from God's name), each word is accompanied by a wave. The *lulav* and *etrog* are also waved when the Hebrew words *Ana Adonai Hosheeya Na* ("Deliver us God, we implore You") are recited. With the exception of the word *Adonai* (God), the *lulav* and *etrog* are waved twice on each of the words *Ana*, *Hosheeya*, and *Na*. According to the Talmud (*Sukkah* 37b), we wave toward the four points of the world in honor of God to Whom the four corners of the world, upwards and downwards, heaven and earth, belong, proclaiming thereby that the world is God's and that God's dominion is everywhere.

Also, we wave the four species to and fro to ward off harmful winds, upwards and downwards to keep away harmful waters. The ceremony thus becomes a form of prayer through action, recalling the agricultural theme of the festival.

Torah and *Haftarah* Summaries

After the *Hallel* service, two Torah scrolls are removed from the Ark. Following is a summary of the Torah readings and *Haftarot* for the first two days of Sukkot.

Torah reading for the first and second days of Sukkot (Leviticus 22:26–23:44): The reading for the first two days of Sukkot contains a comprehensive description of the sacred seasons of the Jewish year, and, of course, includes the festival of Sukkot.

Haftarah of First Day Sukkot (Zechariah 14): Taken from the last chapter of the Book of Zechariah, the *Haftarah* is a vision of God's judgment upon the enemy nations. Israel will finally be redeemed from the hands of its many enemies. At that time the nations will be converted to the worship of the one God of Israel, and Jerusalem will be elevated into the religious center of the world. Tradition has it that the final judgment described in this *Haftarah* will take place on the festival of Sukkot, and thus its link to the holiday.

Haftarah for the Second Day of Sukkot (1 Kings 8:2–21): The *Haftarah* tells of the dedication of the Jerusalem Temple by King Solomon in the tenth century B.C.E. The consecration of the Temple was celebrated by festivities extending over fourteen days, of which the last seven were the festival of Sukkot. Thus, the choice of this passage.

Torah Reading for the Intermediate Sabbath of Sukkot (Exodus 33:12–34:26): The episode of the golden calf created a rift between God and the Israelites. Moses begs for forgiveness, and, in this Torah reading, God instructs Moses to hew another set of stone tablets to replace the first that he had broken. At the second revelation God makes known his thirteen Divine attributes, which include mercy, graciousness, patience, generosity, truth, and forgiveness. God renews His covenant with the Israelites, reminding them that they must reject idolatry and worship only Him.

Haftarah of the Intermediate Sabbath of Sukkot (Ezekiel 38:18–39:16): Taken from the Book of Ezekiel, the *Haftarah* in the main is a prophecy of the messianic time to come. The Prophet Ezekiel foretells that the restoration of Israel to the land of its ancestors will include battles and invasions under the leadership of God, an apocalyptic figure of unknown identity. An old tradition to the effect that this battle will be waged during Sukkot determined the choice of this *Haftarah* for the intermediate Sabbath of Sukkot.

Hoshannot

Special prayer-poems known as *Hoshannot* are recited during the festival of Sukkot after the additional *Musaf* service. They are essentially pleas for deliverance and liberation and were composed by Rabbi Elazar ha-Kallir, who presumably lived in Israel during the eighth century. The *Mishnah* (*Sukkah* 4:5) describes the encircling of the altar with willow branches in the Temple:

> How was the *mitzvah* of the willow performed? There was a place below Jerusalem called Motza. They descended

there, gathered from there large willow branches, and
came and stood them up against the sides of the altar,
with their tops drooping over the top of the altar . . .
Each day they would circle the altar one time and say,
Ana Adonai Hosheeya na—"Please, God, bring salvation now . . ."

Alphabetically arranged, each of the *Hoshannot* com-
positions contain as many verses or phrases as there are
letters in the Hebrew alphabet. They are replete with
historical and midrashic allusions and are constructed in
an involved poetic fashion. They consist of many intri-
cate acrostics and a large variety of Hebrew synonyms.
One of the *Hoshannot*, for example, is composed of an
interesting alphabetical list of twenty-two Hebrew synonyms referring to the Temple at Jerusalem. Another
presents an alphabetical description of the qualities
attributed to the people of Israel in Jewish literature. A
third enumerates destructive forces of nature, such as
locusts, mentioned in the Bible on various occasions.
During the weekday *Hoshannot*, a Torah scroll is removed from the Ark and the Ark is left open. The reader
takes the *etrog* and *lulav* and chants four introductory
verses, each beginning with *hosha na* ("save us"). The
congregation repeats each verse after the reader. Then a
procession of all who have an *etrog* and *lulav* is formed,
and it follows the reader around the sanctuary while the
congregation and the reader responsively recite the
hymn for the day. When Sukkot falls on the Sabbath,
the *Hoshannot* are recited but there is no procession
with *lulav* and *etrog*.

The Intermediate Days of Sukkot

On Sukkot there are five intermediate days. The observance of eating in the *sukkah* and the benediction over
the *etrog* and *lulav* apply as on the first two days. The
complete *Hallel* is recited each day, and the Torah is read
as well, with the reading consisting of the special
sacrifices that were offered in biblical times during
Sukkot (Numbers 29:17–34).

It is customary to read the Book of Ecclesiastes on the
Sabbath of the Intermediate days. Although the mood of
the Book is cynical, it does teach that one should be
content with one's lot, that there is no joy in the
possession of material wealth, and that everything we
have is a gift from God. These themes reflect the mood
of the festival. Following is a brief excerpt from Chapter
3 of the Book of Ecclesiastes. These words were re-
corded several decades ago by a group called the Birds,
who turned them into a hit song called "Turn, Turn
Turn":

To everything there is a season, and a time to every
   purpose under heaven:
A time to be born, and a time to die;
A time to plant, and a time to pluck up that which is
   planted.
A time to kill, and a time to heal;
A time to break down, and a time to build up.
A time to weep and a time to laugh;
A time to mourn and a time to dance.
A time to cast away stones, and a time to gather stones
   together.

A time to embrace and a time to refrain from embracing.
A time to seek and a time to lose;
A time to keep and a time to cast away.
A time to rend and a time to sew;
A time to keep silent and a time to speak.
A time to love and a time to hate.
A time for war and a time for peace. (Ecclesiastes 3:1–8)

Hoshanna Rabbah

The last of the Intermediate Days, the seventh day of
Sukkot, and officially the last day of the festival, is called
Hoshanna Rabbah. Tradition has made this day into a
sequel to the Days of Awe, lengthening the period of
penitence, postponing the day when final sentence is to
be rendered, and giving an opportunity to those who
have not made full use of the grace afforded by Yom
Kippur. The *Mishnah* designated Hoshanna Rabbah as
the day of striking twigs and relates that "people used to
bring twigs and strike them against the ground at the
sides of the altar" (*Sukkah* 4:6). Kabbalistic influence
gave Hoshanna Rabbah a status akin to that of Yom
Kippur: "The seventh day of the festival is the close of
the judgment of the world, and writs of judgment issue
from the sovereign" (*Zohar, Tzav* 31b). People often
wish each other *pikta tovah*—a good note, meaning a
good writ of judgment on Hoshanna Rabbah.

The synagogue services on Hoshanna Rabbah are
similar to those of the other intermediate days, with
some variations. For example, several psalms that are
recited on Sabbaths and festivals are added. High holiday melodies are often added and in some communities

the custom is to say *ayn keylohenu* at the conclusion of the service.

The main variation comes during the Hoshanna Rabbah service. Whereas on each day of the Sukkot festival one Torah scroll is taken out of the Ark, and one procession is made around the sanctuary, on Hoshanna Rabbah all the Torah scrolls are taken out of the Ark and seven processions are made. Additional hymns, penitential in nature, are then recited. Sephardic communities recite verses after each procession, recalling the seven great personalities of the *ushpizin*, who in mystical circles correspond to the seven divine attributes.

Following is the text of the introductory Hoshanna verses, the Hoshanna paragraph for the seventh circuit, and selected verses following the seventh processional:

For Your sake, our God, save, we beseech You.
For Your sake, our Creator, save, we beseech You.
For Your sake, our Redeemer, save, we beseech You.
For Your sake, O You Who searches us, save we beseech You.
Seventh Procession: For the sake of the patriarch Abraham cast into the flames of fire. For the sake of Isaac, his son, bound on the wood for the fire. For the sake of Jacob, the mighty, who wrestled with a prince of fire. For the sake of Israel's hosts whom You did lead by cloud and light of fire. For the sake of Moses taken up on high and exalted as the angels of fire. For the sake of Aaron, Your minister, among the hosts of fire. For the sake of the Ten Commandments, a gift from out of fire. For the sake of the tabernacle covered by curtains and cloud of fire. For the sake of Mount Sinai whereon You did come down in fire. For the sake of the beloved

shrine which You did love more than the heavens of fire;
for the sake of Moses who remained in prayer until the
sinking of the fire. For the sake of Aaron who took the
censer and allayed Your wrath of fire. For the sake of
Phineas who flamed with zeal as of fire. For the sake of
Joshua who at the wave of whose hand there descended
stones of fire. For the sake of Samuel who placed on the
altar a suckling lamb as an offering burned by fire. For
the sake of David who stood at the threshing floor and
won grace by fire. For the sake of Solomon who prayed
in the Temple court until there descended fire. For the
sake of Elijah, Your messenger, taken by chariot and
horses of fire. For the sake of three holy men cast into a
furnace of fire. For the sake of Daniel who beheld
myriads of angels and streams of fire. For the sake of the
desolations of Your city burned by fire, O save, we
beseech You. For the sake of the generations of princes
of Judah whom You will make as a refining furnace of
fire, O save, we beseech You.

Savior of mighty ones that dwelt with You,
In Lud, the land whence You did set them free.
So save You us.
As You did save together God and nation,
The people singled out for God's salvation.
So save You us.
The hosts of Your redeemed, with manifold
Angelic hosts were saved by You of old.
So save You us . . .
Your Ark was won by marvels from the enemy,
Philistia, sinful, by Your wrath laid low.
So save You us.
And with Your banished throngs to Babylon
Journeyed in love Your Presence, Gracious One.

So save You us.
Helper of Jacob's captive tribes of yore,
Return, and Jacob's exiled tents restore.
So save You us.
For those who kept Your law and hoped for Your
    salvation,
God, You have ever been the savior of our nation.
And save You us.
God, save, we beseech You.

During these prayers the *etrog* and *lulav* are taken aside and the *hoshanna*, consisting of five willow twigs tied together, is held in hand. The text from the *siddur* continues as follows:

Give rain. Your lieges pour their hearts as water. O save us. For Abram's sake who went through fire and water. O speed us. In courtesy, he gave the angels water. O save us, mighty God. Give rain. For us to pass was cleft the water. O save us. For Isaac's sake on mountain bound for slaughter, O speed us. He turned and dug his people wells of water. O save us. Give rain. We are the pure who camped by water. O save us. For Jacob's sake who set the rods in water, O speed us. He strained and rolled the stone from off the water. O save us. Give rain. Blest heirs to Torah's quickening water. O save us. Because of those who digged with staves for water, O speed us. To win for them and for their offspring water. O save us. Give rain. Today as we cry for water. O save us. For Moses's sake who found his people water. O speed us. He smote the rock and lo, out gushed the water. O save us. Give rain. Our sires sang round the well of water. O save us. Because of Moses at Meribah's water. O speed us. At Your command he gave the thirsting water. O save us. Give rain. Your holy servants poured You water. O save us. For Your chief minstrel's sake who longed for water. O Save us. Yet turned and made libation with the water. O save us. Give rain. Four plants we wave that love the water. O Save us. For Zion's sake, the home of living water, O speed us. The parched earth open to the heavens' water . . . Hark, the heralding of good tidings.

At the end of the service, worshipers strike the willows against the ground or against other solid objects and the following supplication is said:

Our God and God of our ancestors, You have chosen our true prophets and their good ways. In Your compassionate favor may it be Your will to accept our prayer and the circuits we have made. Recall for us the merit of Your seven devotees and free us from the sins which divide us from You. Hear our cry that we may be sealed for good. O You who suspends the world in space, seal us for good in the book of life.

May Your fulfillment of Your command to take the willow and the *lulav* cluster help us to attain recognition of Your Divine Presence among us. Look with absolving grace on Your servants. Pardon our weaknesses and receive us in our contrition for failures. Open Your goodly treasure to satisfy our thirsting soul, even as it is written in Your Torah, May God open for you His goodly treasure, the heavens, to give you rain in its season for your lands, and to bless all the work of your hand. Save Your people and bless Your heritage, and tend them and sustain them forever. May these my words wherewith I have entreated before God be nigh to God day and

night, so that God shall maintain the cause of His servant
and of His people Israel day by day, that all the peoples
of the earth may know that the Lord He is God, there is
none else.

The beating of the willows may be explained in this
way. These branches, when shaken or struck, lose their
leaves one after the other. So do the trees from which the
branches have been cut, and so also all other trees. But
the rain and heat sent by God in due time give them
fresh life, and they produce new leaves. Our experience
is similar. The struggle for life reduces our strength and
weakens our health. But faith in God and trust in God's
providence renew our strength. Our health improves,
our cares and troubles are diminished, and we feel
ourselves restored to fresh life.

Others explain that the leaves falling off symbolizes
the separation of sin from one's life.

Because of the penitential nature of the day, the
service leader wears a white robe (*kittel*) during the
service, as on Yom Kippur. It is also a well-established
custom to spend the preceding night in study, as on the
first day of Shavuot.

Laws, Symbolism, and Assembly of the Four Species

The Bible's instruction regarding the ritual of the *arba'ah minim*—the four species—is as follows:

> On the fifteenth day of the seventh month when you have gathered in the fruits of the land, you shall keep the Feast of the Lord seven days. You shall take unto yourselves on the first day the fruit of goodly trees, branches of the palm trees, boughs of thick trees and willows of the brook, and you shall rejoice before God for seven days." (Leviticus 23:39–41)

What exactly is the "fruit of a goodly tree"? What precisely are "boughs of thick trees"? The Bible does not explain. Here again their identifications are a matter of tradition handed down from generation to generation.

The fruit of the goodly trees is identified as the *etrog* (citron). Branches of palm trees, the *lulav*; the boughs of thick trees, the myrtle (*hadas*); willows of the brook, twigs of the willow tree (*aravot*).

For the observant Jew, part of the annual rites of fall is the search for an *etrog*. According to Jewish law, an *etrog* must be completely clean. Even a slight scratch or blemish on the skin of the fruit may render it unusable. Its skin should be textured with bumps and ridges, not smooth like a lemon, and its shape should be as a tower, wide at its base and growing narrower as it reaches the flowering head, or *pitam*. In addition, there are factors of individual taste that come into play. While the Ashkenazi, or European Jew, seems to prefer a slimmer variety of the fruit, Jews from North Africa and the Middle East often favor the large, plump *etrog*. Although tradition regards the *pitam* as the beauty of the fruit, some consumers specifically prefer a *pitam*less *etrog*. To prevent the *etrog* from being damaged, etrog holders have existed as a form of Jewish art for centuries.

The myrtle and the willow leaves are placed in a Y-shaped basket-like holder that serves to keep them together. There are numerous rabbinic interpretations of the *lulav* and *etrog* that have developed over the centuries. Following is a cross section of laws related to the Four Species, as culled from the Code of Jewish Law (condensed version).

1. It is an established custom in Israel that if one buys an *etrog* and a *lulav* and is not sure whether or not they are valid, one should show them to a rabbi to ascertain their validity, for there are conflicting opinions regarding the same. An effort should be made to purchase a fresh *lulav*, because a dry *lulav* is acceptable only in an emergency. Some authorities hold that if a *lulav* has no more green in it, it is considered dry. The required length

of a *lulav* is that its stock, besides its fronds, should measure four hand-breadths (sixteen inches).

2. The *hadas* (myrtle) should be three-leaved, that is, there should be three leaves around the twig, neither one higher or lower than the others. Also, the leaves should cover the wood, that is, the top of the lower group of leaves should cover over the stems of the upper leaves. One who fears the word of God should endeavor to purchase fresh and green *hadassim* that are three-leaved and beautiful. If they have been raised locally, he should investigate whether or not they have been grafted and whether they grew in a pot having no aperture at the bottom. The same investigation should be made about the *lulavim* that grow in our regions.

3. The requisite length of a *hadas* is three hand-breadths. The entire *hadas*, from the bottom to the top, should be three-leaved.

4. One must make sure that the tops of the *hadasim* are not broken off. But if one has only *hadasim* with clipped tops, one should consult a scholar. However, the small twigs that grow between the stems should be pulled off, so that they do not separate the stems.

5. The *aravah* (willow branch) is recognizable by its leaves, which are lengthy, with a smooth edge, and by its red stem. Even while the *aravah* is still green, it is valid, inasmuch as it turns red when on the tree. Most of this kind grow by brooks, and therefore are called willows of

the brook. The requisite size of the *aravah* is the same as that of the *hadas*.

6. An *aravah* that is dried up, or from which most of the leaves have fallen off, or from which the top of the stem is broken off is invalid. Some authorities hold that if the leaves have been partly detached and are dangling, the *aravah* is invalid. Special care should be taken of the *aravah*, for at times the leaves fall off, either because of its friction with the *lulav*, or because of the waving, and then it is rendered invalid.

7. A Jew should not personally cut from the tree any of the four species for his own use, even if the owner of the ground grants him permission. But a non-Jew or another Jew should cut them and then the Jew should purchase it from him.

8. We take three *hadas* twigs and two *aravah* twigs and bind them together with the *lulav*, so that they form a single fascicle. We must take care to bind them together in the way they grow, with the cut edges downward. The *hadas* should be bound on the right side of the stem of the *lulav*, and the *aravah* on the left; that is, when taking the *lulav* with its back toward us, the *hadas* should be toward our right hand, and the *aravah* toward our left. At the bottom they should all be even, so that by taking the *lulav* we could grasp all the species. Nevertheless, we should see that the *hadas* is somewhat higher than the *aravah* and be careful that the stock of the *lulav* is at least one hand-breadth higher than the *hadas*. They should be bound together with a perfect

knot, that is, two knots, one on top of the other. Besides
binding these species together, three more bands should
be placed on the *lulav*, but the space on one hand-
breadth at the top of the *lulav* should be left without a
band, so that it might rustle when it is waved.

9. One who does not possess a choice set of the four
species should rather fulfill the precept with a set
belonging to his friend.

10. A left-handed person should take the *lulav* in the
left hand and the *etrog* in the right hand. If he has done
the opposite, he should take them again without saying
a benediction. A person who is ambidextrous is considered to be like any other ordinary person.

11. It is permissible to put the *lulav* back in water
during the festival and add water to it, but one must not
change the water. However, during the intermediate
days of the festival, it is imperative to change the water
so that the *lulav* remains fresh and bright.

12. During the seven days of Sukkot, even on the
Sabbath, it is forbidden to sniff the aroma of the *hadas*.
But the aroma of the *etrog* may be sniffed on the
Sabbath, saying the benediction, "Who put a good odor
in fruit." During the other days of the festival, the aroma
of the *etrog* should not be scented, even when it is not
taken to fulfill the precept with it. The *lulav* may not be
handled on the Sabbath. However, the *etrog*, the fragrance of which may be scented on the Sabbath, may be
handled.

13. If two persons buy an *etrog* and the other species in partnership, it is presumed that they are buying it with the intention of mutually transferring their share in it to each other when each performs the precept with it. Hence, it is customary for a congregation to buy an *etrog* for all the congregants, and whoever can afford it should pay something for it. Yet it is best to perform the precept with an *etrog* belonging to an individual if it and the other species are of standard quality, for whatever an individual transfers to his neighbor is more preferable.

A variety of symbolic interpretations of the four species have been offered. Following are some of the symbolic interpretations of the four species in rabbinic thought:

1. **Beauty of the Four Species:** According to the *Sefer HaHinnuch*, the four species naturally cause man joy by virtue of their beauty. Thus, God commanded that we take and use them during the festival of our joy.

2. **Joy and the Four Species:** Maimonides, in his *Guide for the Perplexed*, writes as follows:

> The fours species are a symbolic expression of our rejoicing over the Israelites as having emerged from the wilderness, "not a place of seed, figs, vines, or pomegranates, and without water to drink" (Numbers 20:5), to a country full of fruit trees and rivers. In order to remember this, we take the most pleasant fruit of the land, the best-smelling branches, the most beautiful leaves, and also the best of herbs, or the willows of the

brook. These four species also have these three virtues: First, they were plentiful in the Land of Israel, so that everyone could easily get them. Secondly, they have a pleasant appearance; some of them, the *etrog* and the myrtle, are also excellent as regards their aroma, the branches of the palm tree and the willow having neither good nor bad smell. Thirdly, they keep fresh and green for seven days, which is not the case with pomegranates and the like.

3. **Mitzvah for the Sake of Heaven:** The initials of the word *etrog* represent the verse "*al tevoaynee regel ga'avah*"—bring me not to the point of arrogance (Psalms 36:12), the implication being that the *etrog* figuratively pleads with its owner that he not become arrogant by virtue of his owning a beautiful, costly *etrog*. Instead, let him perform the mitzvah totally for the Sake of Heaven (Baal Shem Tov).

4. **Human Body:** The rabbis compare the four species with parts of the human body to which they are similar in shape:

the *lulav* represents the spine

the *etrog* represents the heart

the myrtle represents the eyes

the willow represents the lips.

By bringing together these four plants that symbolize four body parts in man, man unites his body in the service of God.

5. **Four Types of Jews:** Just as the *etrog* has taste as well as fragrance, so the Jews have among them those who possess learning as well as good deeds. As the *lulav* has taste but not fragrance, so the Jews have among them those who possess learning without good deeds. As the myrtle has fragrance but not taste, so the Jews have among them those who possess good deeds but not learning. As the willow has neither fragrance nor taste, so the Jews have among them those who possess neither good deeds nor learning. What does the Holy Blessed One do to them? He says, "Let them all be tied together in one band, and they will atone one for another." (Leviticus Rabbah 30)

6. **The Human Body and the Four Species:** The *etrog* is similar to the heart and atones for the heart's evil thoughts. The myrtle is similar to the eyes and atones for the evil sights that the eyes seek; as it is said: "And you shall stray after your hearts and after your eyes." The willow is similar to the lips and atones for the expressions of the lips. The *lulav* has only one heart, and so does Israel have only one heart, for their Father in Heaven (Anaf Yosef).

7. **The Four Species and Biblical Personalities:** In elaborating on several rabbinic traditions, the commentator Bachya ibn Asher says that the *etrog* can be compared to Abraham because it is a beautiful fruit. Abraham's old age was beautiful. Isaac can be compared to the *lulav* by the wordplay on the word *kappot* ("branches"), as well as by stemming from a root that

means "to bind." The *lulav* has branches, and Isaac was bound and ready to be offered as a sacrifice. Jacob is like the myrtle, which is thick with leaves, symbolizing Jacob's being blessed with many children. Finally, Joseph can be compared to the willow, which dries up quickly, since he died before all of his brothers (Bachya ibn Asher).

8. **The Four Species as the Four Kingdoms:** The four species remind us of the four kingdoms that caused Jews to suffer—Babylonia, Persia, Greece, and Rome. Just as the Jewish people survived these political forces, so, too, with God's help, they shall survive others in the future.

9. **The *Lulav* and Life:** In *gematriah* (Jewish numerology), the Hebrew word *lulav* has the value of 68, which is the same numerical value of the Hebrew word *chayim*, meaning life (Rabbi Yehuda Aryeh Leib of Ger).

Assembling the Four Species

Following are the instructions for the assembly of your own *lulav*:

1. Place the *lulav* in the Y-shaped holder.

2. Carefully place three myrtle leaves on the right and two willow twigs in the left part of the Y-shaped holder with the spine of the *lulav* facing you as the *lulav* is placed in the central part of the holder.

3. Take several leaves off of the *lulav* and tie them in a bow in three places along the length of the *lulav*.

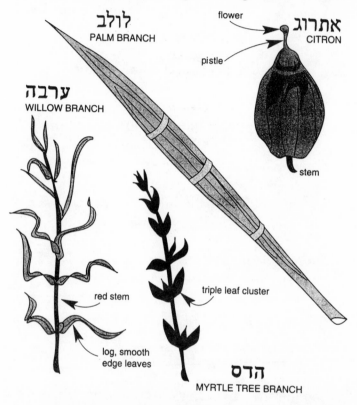

לולב
PALM BRANCH

flower

אתרוג
CITRON

pistle

ערבה
WILLOW BRANCH

stem

red stem

triple leaf cluster

log, smooth
edge leaves

הדס
MYRTLE TREE BRANCH

LAWS AND SYMBOLISM OF THE SUKKAH

The *sukkah* is the Hebrew word for the booth erected for the festival of Sukkot, in accordance with the biblical commandment "You shall dwell in booths seven days" (Leviticus 23:42). The reason for the commandment given in the Bible is "that your generations may know that I made the children of Israel to dwell in booths, when I brought them out of the land of Egypt" (Leviticus 23:43). Since the Israelites in the desert dwelt in tents and not in booths, the Talmud records a dispute between Rabbi Eliezer and Rabbi Akiva on whether the *sukkot* in Leviticus 23:43 were actual or metaphorical booths, the latter referring to the protective "clouds of glory" (Talmud, *Sukkah* 11b) that accompanied the Israelites throughout.

Details of the construction of the *sukkah* are discussed in the talmudic tractate of *Sukkah*. Following are some of the important laws and rulings related to the *sukkah* as culled from rabbinic rulings in the Talmud and the Code of Jewish Law:

Building a *Sukkah*

1. According to Bet Shammai, the *sukkah* must be large enough to contain a man's head, most of his body, and his table (Talmud, *Sukkah* 2:7).

2. The walls of the *sukkah* may be made of any material, but must be sturdy enough to withstand an ordinary wind (Talmud, *Orach Chayim* 630:10).

3. It is meritorious to start building the *sukkah* immediately after Yom Kippur, even if it is Friday, because a chance to perform a precept should not be put off. One should choose for it a clean site. Everyone should build the *sukkah*, even if one is an eminent person (Code of Jewish Law, Condensed Version, Chapter 134).

4. There are many different opinions regarding the roofing of the *sukkah*. However, since we generally

cover it with the branches of trees, or with reeds, which are detached products of the soil and not subject to defilement and are not tied together, there is no cause for scruples (Code of Jewish Law, Condensed Version, Chapter 134).

5. Enough boughs should be placed upon the *sukkah* so as to have more shade than sun. If it has more sun than shade, it is invalid. It is therefore necessary to put on enough branches, so that even if they should dry up, there would still be more shade than sun (Code of Jewish Law, Condensed Version, Chapter 134).

6. A *sukkah* that is erected underneath the branches of a tree is invalid. Even if the branches by themselves would provide more sun than shade, and the *sukkah* has been adjusted by means of putting thereon extra branches, it is, nevertheless, invalid (Code of Jewish Law, Condensed Version, Chapter 134).

7. The obligation may be fulfilled with a borrowed *sukkah* but not with one that is stolen. Hence, a *sukkah* may not be erected on a public place. In an emergency, however, when one has no other *sukkah* available, one may sit in such a *sukkah* and say the prescribed benediction (Code of Jewish Law, Condensed Version, Chapter 134).

Dwelling in the *Sukkah*

1. It is obligatory to eat in the *sukkah* on the first night of the festival (Code of Jewish Law, *Orach Chayim* 639:3).

2. For sleeping, even for a mere nap, a *sukkah* is required. Such is the practice of those who are meticulous in the observance of precepts. Nowadays, however, many people are lax as regards sleeping in the *sukkah*, and the latter authorities, of blessed memory, have advanced some reasons in justification of this latitude (Code of Jewish Law, Condensed Version, Chapter 135).

3. If it rains, one is exempt from staying in the *sukkah*. To release a person from staying in the *sukkah*, it must rain so hard that the food might be spoiled by the rain, or if he estimates that if it had rained that way in his room in the house he would leave it and go into another room, then he may leave the *sukkah* and go into the house. If the weather is so cold that the food congeals, one is exempt from staying in the *sukkah*, and one may eat the meals in the house (Code of Jewish Law, Condensed Version, Chapter 135).

4. With regard to sleep, even a slight rain causes discomfort and one is permitted to leave the *sukkah* because of that. If one has left the *sukkah* because of rain and has gone to sleep in the house, and then the rain ceased, one is not put to the trouble of going back to the *sukkah*, but one may sleep in the house the rest of the night (Code of Jewish Law, Condensed Version, Chapter 135).

5. A sick person and his attendants are exempt from dwelling in the *sukkah*. However, if the invalid is not critically ill, the attendants are exempt only when he needs them. If, however, the invalid is critically ill, they

are exempt even when he does not need them so urgently (Code of Jewish Law, Condensed Version, Chapter 135).

6. After the first night, if the *sukkah* causes one distress because of its cold or windy condition, or because of a bad odor, one is exempt from dwelling in the *sukkah*.

7. One should treat the *sukkah* with the greatest respect and endeavor to adorn it as much as possible. One's finest table utensils should be used in the *sukkah* (Code of Jewish Law, *Orach Chayim* 639:1).

Symbolism of the *Sukkah*

Throughout the centuries, many interpretations have been offered for the *sukkah* and the commandment to dwell therein. Here are some of these interpretations:

1. The *sukkah* was built to show misfortune at a time of good fortune and to remind the rich of the poor (Philo).

2. The *sukkah* serves as an admonition to man not to become overconfident because of affluence. Like one's ancestors in the desert who dwelt in a *sukkah*, one's survival is contingent upon the grace of the Almighty (Rashbam, Leviticus 23:43).

3. Man must leave his permanent home and move into a temporary abode that is devoid of wealth and

security to remind him that he depends upon the Almighty (*Menorat HaMaor*).

4. The *sukkah* is built after Yom Kippur. The Almighty sits in judgment on Rosh Hashanah. On Yom Kippur He seals the verdict. If they were sentenced to go into exile, they build a *sukkah* wherein they dwell and thus are exiled from their homes to the *sukkah*. The Almighty deems it as if they had gone into exile to Babylonia. Thus, the *sukkah* is symbolic of Jewish wandering and homelessness (*Pesikta d'Rav Kahana* 28).

5. The *sukkah* commemorates the first booth built by Abraham when he greeted the three angels (Numbers *Rabbah* 14).

6. The mention of the Exodus from Egypt in connection with the *mitzvah* of the *sukkah* implies that the *sukkah* also serves as a memorial to the miracles of the Exodus (*Tur, Orach Chayim* 625).

7. The *mitzvah* of the *sukkah* arouses the desire to rely on the Holy Blessed One, as did our ancestors who departed from Egypt (*Sefat Emet*).

8. The vision of a universal brotherhood is reflected in the *sukkah*, whose door and roof are open.

9. The *sukkah* is also portrayed in the liturgy as a symbol of peace, known in Hebrew as the *sukkat shalom*. For instance, in the prayer *Hashkeevaynu* ("cause us to lie down") the worshiper petitions God to "spread over

us the shelter of Your peace." The prayer concludes with these words: "Praised are You, God, Who spreads a shelter of peace (*sukkat shalom*) over us, over all God's people Israel, and over Jerusalem."

10. An interesting archaeological study was made in Elephanti, Egypt. They found several business contracts describing real estate dealings that included the phrase: "Upon prompt payment I deed you this land." And then this phrase is followed by a second surprising phrase: "This *simcha* with joy, love, and happiness." After a careful study of the comparative language of real estate contracts, scholars have learned that *simcha* in ancient languages has a second meaning, namely, that of "acceptance." Thus, the phrase *zeman simchatenu* might be rendered not "time of rejoicing" but "moment of acceptance." Thus, sitting in the *sukkah* might be Judaism's way of teaching us that we need to recognize that there are parts of life that are flimsy and frail. We need to set aside a special moment to recognize and accept that which is difficult. Reciting the phrase *zeman simchatenu* as part of the Sukkot liturgy is a consciousness-raising device.

How to Build a *Sukkah*

There are a plethora of *sukkah* designs. The following is a building recipe that is simple and easy to follow:

1. Use the back wall of your house or a garage as one of the four walls.

2. Stack two cement blocks in each corner and insert two-by-fours (seven or eight feet long) into the blocks. Connect the two-by-fours with one-by-twos across the middle and the top.

3. Stretch burlap cloth or plastic, or nail some thin plywood over the frame. (Note: one wall can serve as the entrance if it is covered with burlap cloth.)

4. Put one-by-ones running in both directions on the roof and cover with bamboo, twigs, corn husks, or another organic material. Remember to let the stars shine through.

5. Decorate the inside of the *sukkah* with fruit hangings, Rosh Hashanah greeting cards, posters, paper chains, and the like.

6. Hang an electric light fixture in the *sukkah* for dining in the evening.

Sukkah diagram

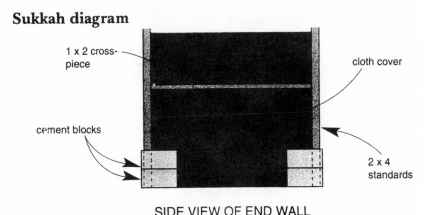

1 x 2 cross-piece

cloth cover

cement blocks

2 x 4 standards

SIDE VIEW OF END WALL

Sukkot Oddities and Curiosities

The following is a cross section of curious and unusual facts related to the festival of Sukkot. They are culled from a variety of Jewish sources.

1. **Season of Our Rejoicing:** Of the three major festivals, Passover, Shavuot, and Sukkot, only Sukkot is designated as *zeman simchatenu*, "the season of our rejoicing." Among the several reasons offered for this designation is that only regarding Sukkot does the Bible specifically command us to rejoice on a festival. In fact, the Bible mentions joy with reference to the festival of Sukkot more frequently than to any other festival: "You shall rejoice before the Lord your God (Leviticus 23:40); "you shall rejoice in your festival" (Deuteronomy 16:14); and "you shall be only joyous" (Deuteronomy 16:15).

2. **Seventy Oxen:** During Temple times, in addition to the regular daily sacrifices, the wine libation, and the

water libations, additional sacrifices were offered each day of Sukkot. As prescribed in the Book of Numbers, Chapter 29, a different number of oxen was offered each day—thirteen on the first day, twelve on the second, with the total decreasing by one on each successive day. The total number of oxen offered throughout the festival came to seventy, corresponding to the seventy nations that descended from Noah and that were the ancestors of all the nations of the world.

3. **Hebrew Letters and the Construction of the Sukkah:** The Chida perceived the Hebrew letters סכה, *sukkah*, to allude to laws of construction of a *sukkah:*

ס Scrupulous people build a *sukkah* enclosed by walls on all sides, like the completely enclosed letter ס.

כ Some construct only three walls, like the letter כ, which is also permissible.

ה It is also permissible to construct one of two walls and a third partial unattached wall, like the letter ה.

4. **The *Sukkah* and the Land of Israel:** The great scholar the Vilna Gaon observes that there are two religious obligations that the Jew observes by entering with his entire being: dwelling in a *sukkah* and in the land of Israel. An allusion to this thought is found in Psalms 76:3: "In Shalem [i.e., Jerusalem, but literally 'whole'] is his *sukkah*, and his dwelling place in Zion." The Vilna Gaon explained the passage this way: "Man is whole when he is in God's *sukkah*, and likewise when his dwelling place is in Zion."

5. **Kissing the *Sukkah*:** It is the practice of spiritually exalted people to kiss the *sukkah* both before entering and leaving to demonstrate their love of the *mitzvah* (*Ba'er Heitev*, paragraph 677, citing *Shelach*).

6. **The *Etrog*—A *Mitzvah* for the Sake of Heaven:** The initials of the word *etrog* represent the verse *al tevoaynee regel ga'avah*—"bring me not to the point of arrogance" (Psalms 36:12). The implication is that the *etrog* figuratively pleads with its owner that he not become arrogant by virtue of his owning a beautiful, costly *etrog*. Instead, let him perform the *mitzvah* totally for the sake of Heaven (Baal Shem Tov).

7. **Sukkot Allusions:** The mystics observe that the three *hadassim* (willow branches) allude to the three patriarchs—Abraham, Isaac, and Jacob. The two *aravot* (myrtle branches) allude to Moses and Aaron. The *lulav* (palm branch) alludes to Joseph, and the *etrog* alludes to King David (*Leviticus Rabbah* 30:10).

8. **"Fragrant Children":** According to the Talmud (*Menachot* 27a), pregnant women who eat the *etrog* will have fragrant children.

9. **A Hoshanna Rabbah Women's Custom:** According to one tradition, the *etrog*, not the apple, was the fruit eaten by Adam and Eve in the Garden of Eden. There was a custom for women to bite the *pitam* off the *etrog* after services on Hoshanna Rabbah, when the *etrog*'s ritual had ceased. In this way women would symbolically demonstrate that, unlike Eve, they had resisted the

temptation to eat the *etrog* until it was no longer needed for Sukkot. The *pitam* on the *etrog* was placed under the pillow of or near a woman in difficult labor in order to ease the pain.

10. **The Torah Names for the Festival of Sukkot:** The Torah designated four names for the festival of Sukkot: *Chag Ha'asif*—the festival of the ingathering of crops (Exodus 26:16); *Chag Hasukkot*—the festival of booths (Leviticus 23:24); *Chag Adonai*—the festival of the Lord (Leviticus 23:29); and *Hachag*—the festival (i.e., the festival par excellence, connoting its preeminence in the cycle of the Jewish year) (1 Kings 8:2).

11. **Return of the Cloud of Glory:** According to the calculations of the great scholar the Vilna Gaon, the protective cloud of glory was taken away from Israel. On the first day of Sukkot, it was returned, adding yet another reason for the joy of the festival.

12. **The Easy *Mitzvah* of the *Sukkah*:** The Talmud (*Avodah Zarah* 3a) records that in the World to Come, when the Holy Blessed One castigates the gentile nations for not accepting the Torah, they will reply, "Offer us the Torah anew and we will obey it." To test them, God will say, "I have an easy *mitzvah* [i.e., easy, because it is inexpensive to perform] called *sukkah*, go and perform it."

Immediately, every gentile will go and make a *sukkah* on his roof, but God will cause the sun to blaze on them and each of them will kick over his *sukkah* and go away.

13. **Exemptions Due to Distress:** According to the
Talmud, *Sukkah* 26a, if one is distressed in the *sukkah*
due to such conditions as rain or cold, he is exempt from
the *mitzvah*. Such an exemption is unique to the *sukkah*,
appearing nowhere else. According to the Chiddushei
HaRim, a distressed person is exempt from the *mitzvah*
of the *sukkah* because a distressed person loses compo-
sure and presence of mind, and the religious obligation
of the *sukkah* must be performed with full awareness of
its symbolic lesson.

14. **Yuchi Indians Observe Sukkot:** The Yuchi Indian tribe of Oklahoma celebrate an eight-day festival
that bears an amazing resemblance to the Jewish festival
of Sukkot. The Yuchis begin their festival on the day of
the full moon during the holy harvest month. Like the
Jews, they, too, dwell in booths that are covered by
branches and foliage. In the Yuchi processional around
the fire in the holy cultic area, they carry a large
foliage-crested branch. During the celebration, these
branches are shaken, much like the shaking of the four
species.

15. **The Lubavitcher *Chassidim Sukkah*mobile:**
The Lubavitcher *chassidim* each year create a *sukkah* on
wheels, mounted on a large truck. The truck tours the
City of New York during the intermediate days of
Sukkot, allowing Jewish passersby an opportunity to
enter the *sukkah* and recite the blessing over the *lulav*
and *etrog*.

16. **Rain and Eating in a *Sukkah*:** According to
rabbinic law, one is exempted from eating in a *sukkah*

when it is raining. In fact, the tradition denounces those persons who continue to eat in the *sukkah* in the rain. "Whoever is exempt from eating in the *sukkah* and does not go out from the *sukkah*, does not receive a reward for fulfilling a *mitzvah* and is nothing but an ignoramus" (Code of Jewish Law).

17. ***Sukkah* of the Leviathan:** According to Jewish legend, God will make a *sukkah* out of the body of the leviathan (mythical beast) at the end of days and will place the righteous there.

18. A Talmudic Debate: What Is a *Sukkah*?

Rabbi Eliezer and Rabbi Akiva disagree about the interpretation of the biblical verse that states that "you shall live in booths seven days . . ." (Leviticus 23:43). Rabbi Akiva interprets the verse literally—that is, the *sukkot* are huts. Rabbi Eliezer, however, says that the *sukkot* of the verse refer to the clouds of glory that accompanied the Israelites in the desert. Thus, for Rabbi Eliezer, the desert period is marked by God's sheltering presence, sustaining the Israelites with food and water as they marched in the wilderness.

19. **Hoshanna Rabbah and Your Shadow:** According to an old legend, if you see your shadow without a head on the eve of Hoshanna Rabbah, you will die in the coming year. If your shadow has a head, you will live.

20. ***Etrog* Uses:** Some people cover their *etrog* after the festival of Sukkot with cinnamon and let it dry for a few weeks. It can then be used as a spice essence

for *Havdalah. Etrog* jelly is another popular after-the-holiday use for an *etrog*. Here is a recipe for *etrog* jelly:

Ingredients: 1 *etrog*, 2 lemons, 1 cup preserving sugar

a. Slice the fruit into cross sections. Remove the pits and white membranes as much as possible.

b. Place the fruit into a bowl of tepid water for three days. Change the water daily, which removes the bitterness. On the third day, taste the water and if it is not acidic, the fruit is ready.

c. Dry the fruit with a paper towel.

d. Add enough water to the sugar to cover. Cook over a low heat. (Be careful not to burn the sugar.) Add the softened lemon slices and several teaspoons of water. When the sugar is syrupy, add the *etrog*. Continue cooking until the *etrog* gets glossy.

e. Test the jam for a set with a sugar thermometer (about 220°F). As an alternative, take a few small plates. Put them in the freezer for a few minutes with a spoonful of jam on each plate. If the jam puckers and has formed a thick skin when you push it with a spoon, then it is ready. If not, cook it for a few more minutes.

f. Let the jam cool. Then place it in a jar. It should keep for up to two years!

21. **Pizza in the Hut:** Recently in a Central New Jersey Congregation during the intermediate days of Sukkot, the congregation's Jewish Family Matters (in-

volved in creating family programs) served kosher pizza to over 250 satisfied customers. Singing and dancing followed, with additional programs geared to the entire family. Aptly enough, the program was called "Pizza in the Hut!"

22. **A *Lulav* Shake:** In recent years, the United Synagogue of Conservative Judaism in conjunction with the Rabbinical Assembly of America has tried to increase observance of the festival of Sukkot using unique and creative publicity. In one of their more successful campaigns, the advertisement flyer begins by asking the question: "How do you make a *lulav* shake?" (A picture of a milkshake with *lulav* and *etrog* interspersed also appears in the flyer.) The *lulav* shake publicity also includes T-shirts, buttons, and large posters.

23. **Pelted with *Etrogim*:** The Hasmonean king Alexander Yannai, a Sadduccee, was once pelted with *etrogim* while engaged in the sacrifical service. The tragic sequel to this occurrence was that Alexander's soldiers massacred six thousand of the congregants in the Temple (Antiquities 13:13,5).

SUKKOT AND
SHEMINI ATZERET LEGENDS

1. On Sukkot it is customary to invite seven biblical guests into one's own *sukkah*. The custom of inviting these guests (i.e., Abraham, Isaac, Jacob, Joseph, Moses, Aaron, and David) rests on a mystical statement to the effect that the *Shechinah* (Divine Presence) shelters the *sukkah* beneath its wings, and Abraham, in the company of six righteous men, enters to participate in the hospitality of the Jew who properly observes the precept of the *sukkah*. The following legend describes seven groups of righteous people who are worthy of greeting the Divine Presence.

It is written, Let me know the way of life, the fullness of joys in Your Presence (Psalms 16:11). Do not read the Hebrew word in the form whereby it means "fullness" but in the variant form whereby it means "seven."

This is an allusion to the seven groups of righteous people who are worthy of greeting the Divine Presence. These seven groups are differentiated by their appearances. Some resemble the sun, some the moon, some the sky. Some resemble lightning, some the stars. Some resemble roses, and some resemble the *menorah* in the Holy Temple.

. . . The verse concludes, The pleasures of Your right hand are eternal (Psalms 16:11).

Kind David said before the Holy One: "Master of all Worlds, who will tell me which of these groups is the most pleasant and beloved?"

There is a difference of opinion between two *amoraim* about the answer that David received to this question.

One said, "It is the group whose righteousness derives from the study of Torah and the performance of *mitzvot*.

The other said, "It is the group of scribes, teachers of the *Mishnah*, and sincere teachers of small children. These righteous people are destined to reside in the protective shelter at the right of the Eternal One."

Otherwise: It is written, Let me know the way of life, the fullness of joys in Your Presence (Psalms 16:11). This is the voice of the people of Israel speaking to the Holy One.

The people of Israel said, "Let me know the way of life."

The Holy One, Blessed be He, said to them: "Behold, I am giving you the Ten Days of Repentance that begin with Rosh Hashanah and culminate with Yom Kippur."

The people of Israel continued, "The seven joys in Your Presence."

The Holy One, Blessed be He, said to them, "I am giving you seven *mitzvot* during the festival of Sukkot: the four species, the *sukkah*, the festival offering, and the *mitzvah* of being joyful."

What is the meaning of that which is written, "The pleasures of Your right hand are eternal?"

Rabbi Avin said, "This refers to the *mitzvah* of taking the *lulav*, which resembles the spear held aloft by the victor."

There is an analogy to all of this. Two people go before the court to argue their cases against each other. When they emerge, how do we know which one was victorious? The one who is holding the symbolic spear in his right hand is the victorious one.

So, too, do the Jewish people and the peoples of the world argue their cases against each other before the Holy One, Blessed be He, during the days of judgment. When the Jewish people emerge from the days of judgment before the Holy One with their *lulavim* in their right hands on the festival of Sukkot, it becomes clear that they were victorious (*Leviticus Rabbah* 30:2).

2. According to Jewish law, a *sukkah* that is built must be no lower than ten *tefach* measures high. The ancient rabbis hinted at the significance of this rule by telling the following story.

It was taught: Rabbi Yossi says, "The Divine Presence never descended to the lower world, nor did Moses and Elijah ever ascend to the upper world." For it is written, The heavens are the heavens of God, and the earth is given to the people (Psalms 115:16).

How can it be said that the Divine Presence never descended to the lower world? Is it not written, And God came down onto Mount Sinai (Exodus 19:20)?

The Divine Presence hovered ten *tefach* measures above the mountaintop.

Is it not written, And God's feet will stand on that day upon the Mount of Olives (Zechariah 14:14)?

That, too, means ten *tefach* measures above the mountaintop.

How can it be said that Moses and Elijah never ascended to the upper world? Is it not written, And Moses went up to God (Exodus 19:3)?

This means that he stayed within the lowest ten *tefach* measures of the heavens.

And is it not written, And Elijah went up in a storm wind to the heavens (2 Kings 2:11)?

God, too, stayed within the lowest ten *tefach* measures of the heavens.

3. In several places we are reminded in the Talmud that the purpose of the four species is to incur the favor of God in the matter of granting sufficient rainfall. The festival of Sukkot comes in the early autumn at the beginning of the first rainy period in Israel when the earth thirsts for water. The following *midrash* amplifies the purpose of the four species.

It is written, And you shall take for yourselves on the first day the fruit of beautiful trees, branches of palm trees, twigs of myrtle trees, and willows of the brook (Leviticus 23:40).

These four species are symbols for that which is written, Let the field rejoice, and all that are in it, then shall all the trees of the forest sing merrily, before God, for God has come to judge the earth, and He will judge the world with righteousness, and the peoples with His truth (Psalms 96:12–13).

Otherwise: It is written, And you shall take for yourselves on the first day the fruit of beautiful trees . . . (Leviticus 23:40).

Rabbi Hiyya taught: "This verse is telling us that this is

not a collective *mitzvah*. Every single person is required to fulfill the *mitzvah* of taking the four species. It is also telling us that the four species must be of our own property, not of stolen property."

Rabbi Levi said, "If someone comes to fulfill the *mitzvah* with stolen specimens of the four species, to what can he be compared?"

He is comparable to the robber who lurks at the crossroads preying on passersby. One day, one of the emperor's legionnaires who was collecting taxes in that province passed by the crossroads where this robber was lurking. The robber pounced on the legionnaire and took all the money that he had in his possession. The following day the robber was caught and locked in prison. When the legionnaire heard of the robber's arrest, he came to the prison to talk with him.

The legionnaire said, "Give me back everything that you stole from me, and I will speak to the emperor on your behalf."

The robber replied, "I have nothing left from all that I have stolen or bought besides this one small coin that I took from you."

The legionnaire said, "Then give me this small coin, and I will speak to the emperor on your behalf."

The robber extended the coin and said, "Take it,"

The legionnaire took it and said, "Be advised that you are scheduled to be brought to trial before the emperor tomorrow. He will ask you if there is anyone that can speak on your behalf. You are to reply that I can speak on your behalf. He will then summon me, and I will speak on your behalf."

And so it was that the next day the robber was brought to trial before the emperor.

The emperor asked him, "Is there anyone that can speak well of you?"

The robber replied, "There is a certain legionnaire that can speak well of me."

The emperor summoned the legionnaire and asked him, "Do you know anything favorable about this person?"

The legionnaire replied, "I know that when you sent me to collect taxes in that province, this person waylaid me and stole everything that I had. This small coin of mine that I took from him yesterday bears witness to my words."

The startled audience in the courtroom cried out, "Woe to the man whose advocate has become his accuser."

So, too, if a person brings stolen specimens of the four species to incur the favor of the Holy One, Blessed be He, the specimens cry out, "We are stolen, we are stolen."

And the ministering angels gather about and say, "Woe to the person whose advocates have become his accusers" (*Leviticus Rabbah* 30:4–6).

4. The rabbis of old have revealed another symbolic dimension to the four species. They are to serve as reminders of the history of the Jewish people, symbolizing the patriarchs and matriarchs and the illustrious leaders who guided them for many generations. Here is the way that the *Midrash* explains it.

It is written, The fruit of beautiful trees (Leviticus 23:40).

This refers to our ancestor Abraham, whom the Holy One adorned with a ripe old age, as it is written, And

Abraham grew old (Genesis 24:1). The Hebrew usage in this verse is similar to that of the verse: And you shall adorn the face of the old (Leviticus 19:32).

The verse continues, Branches of palm trees (Leviticus 23:40).

The Hebrew word used here for "branches," in a variant form, also means "tied." This is a reference to our ancestor Isaac, who was tied and fettered and offered up as a sacrifice on the altar by his father, Abraham.

The verse then continues, And twigs of myrtle trees (Leviticus 23:40). This refers to our ancestor Jacob who was closely involved with his many children, just as the stalk of the myrtle is tightly wrapped in its leaves.

The verse concludes, And willows of the brook (Leviticus 23:40). This refers to Joseph. Just as the willow is the least durable of the four species, shriveling up before the others, so, too, did Joseph die before the rest of his brothers.

Otherwise: It is written, The fruit of beautiful trees (Leviticus 23:40). This refers to our matriarch Sarah whom the Holy One adorned with a ripe old age, as it is written, And Abraham and Sarah grew old (Genesis 18:11).

The verse continues, Branches of palm trees (Leviticus 23:40). This refers to our matriarch Rebekkah. Just as the palm tree produces edible growths and thorny growths, so, too, did Rebekkah produce a righteous son and an evil son, Jacob and Esau.

The verse continues, And twigs of myrtle trees (Leviticus 23:40). This refers to our matriarch Leah who had many children, just as the myrtle has many leaves.

The verse concludes, And willows of the brook (Leviticus 23:40). This refers to our matriarch Rachel. Just as the willow is less durable than the other species,

being the first to shrivel up, so, too, did Rachel die before
her sister Leah (*Leviticus Rabbah* 30:10).

5. In yet another dimension, the four species are
represented as a cross section of the Jewish people itself.
By gathering all four of the species, the Jewish people
are showing that if all unite in prayer, God will surely
listen to their prayers.

It is written, The fruit of beautiful trees (Leviticus
23:40). This refers to some of the Jewish people. Just as
the *etrog* provides fragrance and food, so, too, are there
some Jewish people who possess Torah and good
deeds.

The verse continues, Branches of palm trees (Leviticus
23:40). This refers to some of the Jewish people. Just as
the palm tree provides food but no fragrance, so, too, are
there some Jewish people who possess Torah but not
many good deeds.

The verse continues, And twigs of myrtle trees (Leviticus 23:40). This refers to some of the Jewish people.
Just as the myrtle tree provides fragrance but no food, so,
too, are there some Jewish people who possess good
deeds but not very much Torah.

The verse concludes, And willows of the brook
(Leviticus 23:40). This refers to some of the Jewish
people. Just as the willow tree provides neither fragrance
nor good, so, too, are there some Jewish people who
possess nothing, neither good deeds nor much Torah.

The Holy One said, "I do not wish to destroy this final
group. Therefore, let all of the groups join together, and
they will atone for each other.

"And if you do so I will Myself ascend, as it is written,

That builds His steps in the heavens and He has established His union on the earth" (Amos 9:6).

Therefore, Moses directed the Jewish people, "And you shall take for yourselves the fruit of beautiful trees" (Leviticus 23:40).

6. The following story provides additional symbolism of the four species.

Like the palm tree that has a single heart that keeps reaching upward toward the heaven, so, too, Israel has a single heart reaching upward to the Heavenly Father.

Of the four plants that constitute the *lulav* cluster, two bear fruit and two do not. Those that bear fruit must be closely tied to the ones that do not bear fruit. The former represent students of the wise whose prayers, in keeping with the warning from Palestine, are meant to bear fruits of mercy for ordinary people. . . . On the other hand, the plants that do not bear fruit must be bound close to those that bear fruit, since the former represent those persons who are meant to provide a shelter of physical comfort for the rabbis and their students. (*Pesikta Rabbati* 51:2)

7. Occasionally, rabbinic texts postulate the medicinal value of the *etrog* as a cure for a disease. The following tale illustrates such a use for an *etrog*.

A tale was told that a certain man had two sons, one of whom was very charitable. The other practiced no charity whatsoever. The son who practiced charity sold his house and all of his other possessions and used the revenue for charity.

Once, on Hoshanna Rabbah, his wife gave him ten

pulsin and said, "Go to the market and buy something for your children." As soon as he went forth, the charity collectors met up with him saying, "Here comes the lord of charity. We implore you to give your share to this charity so that we can buy a wedding dress for a certain orphan girl."

With that he gave the men the ten *pulsin*. Now ashamed to go back to his home, he went to the synagogue where he saw some of the *etrog* fruit that the children are accustomed to throw about on Hoshannah Rabbah. Now we have learned elsewhere that it is permissible to take away the palm branches from children, as well as to eat their *etrogim*. So he took the citrons from them, filled a sack with them and led his wife on a voyage upon the Great Sea, in order to reach the king's province.

Arriving there, it happened that the king was experiencing bowel pain and was told in a dream to eat the *etrogim* that the Jews used in their prayers on Hoshannah Rabbah. If he did this, he would be healed.

They searched all of the ships and all of the province but could not find even a single *etrog*. Finally, they went and found that man sitting on his sack. They asked him, "Do you have anything with you?" He replied, "I am but a poor man, and I have nothing to sell." They searched his sack and found some of the *etrog* fruit. They then inquired, "Where are these from?" The man replied, "They were used by Jews during their prayers on Hoshannah Rabbah." The men then lifted the sack and brought it to the king, who ate the *etrogim* and was thus cured. They emptied the sack and filled it with *denarii*. This confirms the text, For God pays a person according to his actions (Job 34:11). (*Leviticus Rabbah* 37:2)

8. The minor prophet Zechariah describes in his book (Chapter 14) an apocalyptic vision of the salvation of Jerusalem and judgment upon the heathen nations that had attacked her. It will be a final judgment when the nations of the world will be converted to worship God and Jerusalem will be elevated into the religious center of the world as a place of pilgrimage for all nations. Tradition ascribes this final judgment scene as taking place on the Festival of Sukkot. The following legend attempts to explain the biblical verse "In Your right hand there are pleasures of victory" (Psalms 16:11).

> What kind of victory is meant in the verse "In Your right hand there are pleasures of victory?" The kind in which the victor receives a wreath. According to the world's custom, when two charioteers race in the hippodrome, which one of them receives a wreath? The victor. So on New Year's day all the people of the world appear before God like contestants in a parade, including the children of Israel. Then the guardian angels of the world's nations declare, "We were victorious, and in the judgment shall be found righteous." But in reality, no one really knows who was victorious—the children of Israel or the nations of the world.
>
> After New Year's day passes, all the Israelite children come forth on Yom Kippur and fast, dressed in white. But even after the Day of Atonement, no one knows who was victorious.
>
> When the first day of Sukkot arrives, however, all the Israelite children (both grown and little ones), take up their festive wreaths in their right hand and their *etrog* fruit in their left, and then all people of the world truly know that in the judgment the children of Israel were proclaimed victorious. Furthermore, when Hoshannah

Rabbah comes, the Israelites take willows of the brook and circle seven times, while the synagogue reader, like one of God's angels, stands up with the Torah scroll in his arm. The people encircle him, as though he were the altar. And of this circling our rabbis taught: Everyday of the first six days of Sukkot they circled about the altar once, saying, "We beseech You, O God, save us now. We beseech You, O God, make us prosper" (Psalms 118:25).

On the seventh day, they circled around the altar seven times. This circling of the altar is referred to by King David of Israel, in the verse "I will wash my hands in innocence, so, too, will I circle Your altar, O God" (Psalms 26:6).

Then the ministering angels rejoice and say, "The children of Israel are victorious, the children of Israel are victorious." And they also say, "The victory of Israel will not lie nor repent (1 Samuel 15:29). Therefore, David meant to say this: If you perform the rite of the festive wreath known as "a pleasure" and take up the wreath "in your right hand" to praise God, behold, God has made known to you the paths.

Thus David said, "You make me to know the path of life. In Your presence is fullness of joy, in Your right hand are pleasures of victory" (Psalms 16:11).

By the "path of life," David meant New Year's day and the Day of Atonement. By "fullness of joy" he meant the festival of Sukkot. By "in Your presence" David meant Israel's appearance in Jerusalem as stated in the verse "Three times a year all your males shall appear before the Lord your God" (Deuteronomy 16:6). By "in Your right hand are pleasures," David meant the festive wreath [i.e., the *lulav*] called "a pleasure," which is held in the right hand. And by "of victory" King David meant:

I bring to you happy tidings, that at the judgment you are proclaimed victorious over the nations of the world, as it is written, "The victory of Israel will not lie nor repent." (*Midrash* on Psalms 17:5)

9. The rabbinic sages concluded that one must own one's own *lulav* cluster in order to fulfill one's obligation. This decision was based on the biblical verse "And you shall take for you . . ." (Leviticus 23:40). The following story cites an example of the giving of a *lulav* cluster to another to use as a gift.

"And you shall take for you" (Leviticus 23:40). "For you" means "what belongs to you." The rabbis inferred from this verse that no person may fulfill his obligation on the first day of Sukkot with a *lulav* cluster that belongs to another person, unless he later gave it to him as a gift.

Once it happened that Rabbi Gamaliel, Rabbi Joshua, Rabbi Eleazar ben Azariah, and Rabbi Akiva were traveling on a ship, and only Rabbi Gamaliel had a *lulav*, which he had purchased for one thousand *zuzim*. Rabbi Gamaliel took it, fulfilled his obligation, and proceeded to pass it on to Rabbi Joshua as a gift. Rabbi Joshua took it, fulfilled his obligation with it, and gave it to Rabbi Eleazar ben Azariah as a gift. Finally, Rabbi Akiva took it, fulfilled his obligation, and returned it to Rabbi Gamaliel as a gift. (Talmud, *Sukkah* 41b)

10. Shemini Atzeret is often considered a "hold over" festival, appended to the festival of Sukkot. The following tale explains the "hold over" concept in greater detail.

Rabbi Joshua, the son of Levi, said, "It would have been appropriate for the *Atzeret* day of the festival of Sukkot to be fifty days after Sukkot, just as the festival of Shavuot, which is also called *Atzeret*, comes fifty days after the festival of Passover.

"Here is an analogy. A king was celebrating a joyous occasion. He had some married daughters who lived close by and others who lived further away. Those who lived in close proximity were able to leave and come back with ease, but those who lived a great distance could not come and go with such facility.

"The king said to those who lived far away, 'Stay over, and you and I will celebrate for yet one additional day.'

"Since the Passover holiday comes when winter is turning into summer, it comes at a time when the Israelites find it easy to come and go. Therefore, the *Atzeret* day can be fifty days removed from the festival. The holiday of Sukkot, however, comes when the summer is turning to winter. It is a time when it is difficult to travel certain roads, a time of hardship. It is a time when the people of Israel do not find it easy to come and to go. Therefore, the Holy One, Blessed be He, said, 'Stay over, and you and I will celebrate for one additional day.'" (*Pesikta* 30)

11. The following story is another attempt by the rabbis to explain the addition of an eighth day of solemn gathering following the festival of Sukkot.

Rabbi Levi said, What God intended was to give to Israel a festival for every month during the summer. There would be Passover in the month of Nisan, the minor Passover in Iyar, and the holiday of Shavuot in Sivan. But because of the sins and evil deeds that darkened the Israelites' hands when they fashioned the golden calf, God took away the festivals that He had intended for the months of Tammuz, Av, and Elul. God had the following month, Tishri, make up, however, for Israel's being deprived of the festivals that He had intended them to celebrate during the three previous months. Thus, three festivals were presented within the month of Tishri—New Year's to make up for the missing festival in Tammuz, the Great Fast to make up for the missing festival in Av, and the seven days of the Festival of Sukkot to make up for the missing festival in Elul. Then said the Holy One, Blessed be He: Since Tishri makes up for the other months and has not been given a festival that is its own, let it be given its own day. Thus, Israel was charged, "On the eighth day you shall hold a solemn gathering" (Numbers 29:35) (*Pesikta Rabbati* 52:2).

SHEMINI ATZERET

The last two days of Sukkot are called Shemini Atzeret and Simchat Torah. In Israel only one day is celebrated, and it includes the features of both. The *Midrash* gives a poetic touch to the interpretation of Shemini Atzeret. When the children of Israel, after having spent a long holiday period in worship and rejoicing, are about to resume their regular daily life, God says to them: "It is difficult for me to part with you. Tarry a while longer. Stay another day." Hence the name Shemini Atzeret, for the word *atzeret* means "to tarry" or "to hold back" (quoted by Rashi on Leviticus 23:26). A most relevant interpretation of the word *atzeret* is given by Yaakov Zevi Mecklenburg. He asserts that it means "to retain." During the holiday season, we have experienced a heightened religious fervor and a most devout spirit. This last day is devoted to a recapitulation of the message of these days, with the hope that it will be retained the rest of the year.

Since Shemini Atzeret is a separate festival, the obser-

vances that are most characteristic of the Festival of
Sukkot—dwelling in a *sukkah*, the *etrog* and *lulav*, and
the daily procession around the sanctuary—are omitted.

IN THE BIBLE AND THE TALMUD

The biblical source for the festival of Shemini Atzeret is
Numbers 29:35: "On the eighth day you shall hold a
solemn gathering [*atzeret*]. You shall not work at your
occupations. It appears to be a festival that, although
falling on the heels of Sukkot, bears none of its rituals.

The rabbis of the *Midrash* (*Numbers Rabbah* 21)
provide the motive behind this added day of festivities.
During Temple days, the morning devotionals were
inaugurated with a sacrifice called *korban tamid shel
shacharit*. On significant days such as the Sabbath and
other holidays, an additional sacrifice was offered, sig-
nifying the uniqueness of the day. This was known as
korban Musaf, the additional sacrifice. During the seven
days of Sukkot, a total of seventy bullocks were offered,
corresponding to the seventy nations of the world.
During Sukkot, we have prayed for peace and prosper-
ity, not for ourselves alone but for all mankind. On
Shemini Atzeret a single bullock was sacrificed for
Musaf. God speaks to the children of Israel and says,
"Through your sacrifices during the seven days of Sukkot
you have entreated me to bestow My kindness upon all
people. The time has come when you, My people, and I
should celebrate by ourselves, just you and I. You have
offered sacrifices for the benefit of all nations. Now bring
a single bullock as a sacrifice to Me for your own benefit
alone" (*Sefer Ha-Toda'ah*).

IN THE HOME

Shemini Atzeret is a full festival marked by the usual Jewish holiday rituals, including the ritual lighting of candles, the chanting of the festival *Kiddush* over the wine, ritual handwashing, the blessing over the bread, and the blessing after the meal. On the evening of Shemini Atzeret it is customary, before the candlelighting, to light a *Yahrzeit* memorial candle for each deceased family member.

Following is the festival *Kiddush* blessing for Shemini Atzeret. (For other basic blessings you may wish to refer to the Basic Blessings in this volume, pp. 20–27.)

בָּרוּךְ אַתָּה יהוה אֱלֹהֵינוּ מֶלֶךְ הָעוֹלָם, בּוֹרֵא פְּרִי הַגָּפֶן
בָּרוּךְ אַתָּה יהוה אֱלֹהֵינוּ מֶלֶךְ הָעוֹלָם, אֲשֶׁר בָּחַר בָּנוּ מִכָּל-עָם
וְרוֹמְמָנוּ מִכָּל-לָשׁוֹן, וְקִדְּשָׁנוּ בְּמִצְוֹתָיו. וַתִּתֶּן לָנוּ יהוה אֱלֹהֵינוּ
בְּאַהֲבָה (שַׁבָּתוֹת לִמְנוּחָה וּ)מוֹעֲדִים לְשִׂמְחָה, חַגִּים וּזְמַנִּים לְשָׂשׂוֹן,
אֶת-יוֹם (הַשַּׁבָּת הַזֶּה וְאֶת-יוֹם) הַשְּׁמִינִי חַג הָעֲצֶרֶת הַזֶּה, זְמַן
שִׂמְחָתֵנוּ, (בְּאַהֲבָה) מִקְרָא קֹדֶשׁ, זֵכֶר לִיצִיאַת מִצְרָיִם. כִּי-בָנוּ
בָחַרְתָּ וְאוֹתָנוּ קִדַּשְׁתָּ מִכָּל-הָעַמִּים, (וְשַׁבָּת) וּמוֹעֲדֵי קָדְשֶׁךָ (בְּאַהֲבָה
וּבְרָצוֹן) בְּשִׂמְחָה וּבְשָׂשׂוֹן הִנְחַלְתָּנוּ. בָּרוּךְ אַתָּה יְיָ, מְקַדֵּשׁ (הַשַּׁבָּת
וְ) יִשְׂרָאֵל וְהַזְּמַנִּים.

Barukh atah adonai eloheinu melekh ha'olam, borei p'ri hagafen. Barukh atah adonai eloheinu melekh ha'olam, asher bεchar banu mikol am v'ro-m'manu mikol lashon v'kid'shanu b'mitzvotav vatiten lanu adonai eloheinu b'ahavah (shabbatot lim'nuchah u) mo'adim l'simchah chagim

uz'manim l'sasson et yom (hashabbat hazeh v'et yom)
hash'mini chag ha'atzeret hazeh, z'man simchateinu
(b'ahavah) mikra kodesh zeikher litzi'at mitzrayim. Ki vanu
vacharta v'otanu kidashta mikol ha'amim (v'shabbat)
umo'adei kodsh'kha (b'ahavah uv'ratzon) b'simchah uv'sas-
son hinchaltanu. Barukh atah adonai, m'kadesh (hashabbat
v') yisra'eil v'haz'manim.

Praised are You, Eternal our God, Sovereign of the Universe
who creates fruit of the vine.
Praised are You, Eternal our God, Sovereign of the Universe
who has chosen and distinguished us from among all
others by adding holiness to our lives with mitzvot. Lovingly
have You given us (Shabbat for rest,) festivals for joy and
holidays for happiness, among them this (Shabbat and
this) day of Shemini Atzeret, season of our joy,a day of
sacred assembly recalling the Exodus from Egypt. Thus
You have chosen us, endowing us with holiness from
among all peoples by granting us (Shabbat and) Your
hallowed festivals (lovingly and gladly) in happiness and
joy. Praised are You, God who hallows (Shabbat and) the
people Israel and the festivals.

IN THE SYNAGOGUE

Synagogue services for Shemini Atzeret are as on the first
two days of Sukkot, with several variations. *Hallel*
Psalms of praise are recited. Two Torah scrolls are
removed from the Ark, and a *Haftarah* prophetic portion, especially chosen for Shemini Atzeret, is chanted.

Following is a brief summary of the Torah reading and *Haftarah* for Shemini Atzeret:

Torah Portion (Deuteronomy 14:22–16:17): The Torah reading, similar to the eighth day of Passover, deals with a variety of biblical laws:

a. Tithes: One-tenth of the yearly farm produce was to be set aside for the sanctuary.

b. Year of release: In every Sabbatical year (i.e., seventh year), money loans were canceled to allow the poor a chance to move out of their poverty.

c. Release of Hebrew slaves: Slaves were given their freedom after six years of continuous service.

d. Observance of the three pilgrimage festivals: Passover, Shavuot, and Sukkot.

Haftarah for Shemini Atzeret (1 Kings 8:54–66): The first section of the 1 Kings 8, describing the dedication of the Temple, is the *Haftarah* for the second day of Sukkot. The closing part of the chapter is the *Haftarah* reading for Shemini Atzeret. In verse 66, there is a specific reference to the "eighth day," and thus its connection to Shemini Atzeret, the so-called eighth day of the festival of Sukkot.

Prayer for Rain: *Tefillat Geshem*

Throughout Sukkot we hint at our desire for rain through such rituals as the water libation practiced in the Temple and the four species, particularly the willow, which represents the association of plant growth and water. Continuing with the water theme, a particular feature of Shemini Atzeret is the prayer for rain, thus officially beginning Israel's rainy season. Since the modern State of Israel relies so heavily on substantial rain for its crops, the prayer for rain is recited with a special plaintive melody, and the cantor dons a white *kittel* (robe), as on Yom Kippur.

The prayer for rain corresponds to the prayer for dew (*tal*) that is said on the first day of Passover. Since the world is judged for rain at this time, according to the Talmud, it is proper to pray for rain at this time of the year. The prayer gives expression to the natural anxiety felt in Israel for the seasonal rain, the absence of which means famine, thirst, and disease. The prayer is delayed until Shemini Atzeret because it should not be invoked when fine weather is needed to enable us to dwell in the *sukkah* (Talmud, *Sukkah* 28b).

The liturgy on Shemini Atzeret introduces the following phrase to be recited henceforth, until Passover, in the *Amidah* prayer—*masheev ha'rua'ch u'moreed hagashem*—"Who causes the wind to blow and the rain to fall."

There are six parts of the prayer for rain, each of which refers to events involving water in the lives of Abraham, Isaac, Jacob, Moses, Aaron, and the Twelve Tribes. Here is a translation of the prayer for rain:

Our God and God of our ancestors:
Remember Abraham who flowed to You like water.
You blessed him like a tree planted by streams of water.

You rescued him from fire and water.

He passed Your test by planting good deeds by every
source of water.

For Abraham's sake, do not keep back water.

Remember Isaac, whose birth was foretold when Abraham
offered the angels a little water.

You asked his father to spill his blood like water.

In the desert Isaac dug and found wells of water.

For Isaac's sake, do not keep back water.

Remember Jacob, who crossed the Jordan's water.

He bravely rolled the stone off the mouth of the well
of water.

He wrestled with an angel made of fire and water,

And therefore You promised to be with him through fire
and water.

For Jacob's sake do not keep back water.

Remember Moses, who was drawn in a reed basket out
of the Nile's water.

Who helped Jethro's daughters: He drew water and gave
the sheep water.

He struck the rock and out came water.

For Moses' sake do not hold back water!

Remember Aaron, the High Priest, who, on Yom Kippur,
washed himself five times with water,

He prayed and was sprinkled with purifying water,

He kept apart from a people who were as unstable as
water.

For Aaron's sake do not hold back water.

Remember the Twelve Tribes whom
You brought through the divided waters;

For whom You sweetened bitter water;
Their descendants' blood was spilled like water.
Turn to us, God, who are surrounded by troubles like
    water.
For the Jewish people's sake, do not hold back water.

You are Adonai, our God
Who causes the wind to blow and the rain to fall.
For blessing and not for curse. Amen.
For life and not for death. Amen.
For plenty and not for lack. Amen.

Simchat Torah

The festival of Simchat Torah (literally, "rejoicing in the Law") is a fitting finale for the fall holiday season. No festival better conveys the Jewish attachment to the Torah than Simchat Torah. In the diaspora it falls on the ninth day of Sukkot and is devoted completely to rejoicing. In Israel, where the eighth day is the last day, the practices of Simchat Torah are observed on Shemini Atzeret.

The name Simchat Torah is not mentioned in the Talmud. In designating the *haftarah* for the day, the Talmud (*Megillah* 31a) refers to it as the second day of Shemini Atzeret. Simchat Torah occurs first in post-geonic literature. Beginning around the tenth century, it began to take on the character of a festival of Torah. The connection to Torah was not based on a historical event but rather on the synagogue liturgy. At this time of year in the fall, the end of the Book of Deuteronomy was read in the synagogue, completing the reading of the entire Torah. On the Sabbath immediately following Shemini

Atzeret, the cycle of Torah reading commenced again with the reading of the opening chapters of the Book of Genesis. To celebrate the completion of the cycle, the festival of Simchat Torah was developed.

In recent years, the Simchat Torah observance has received inspiration from the Jews of the Soviet Union. During the 1960s, Soviet Jews adopted Simchat Torah as their special day of celebration, and among many Russian Jews it became more widely observed than even Passover or Yom Kippur.

IN THE HOME

The home ritual for Simchat Torah, like that of Shemini Atzeret, includes the ritual lighting of candles, the chanting of the festival *Kiddush* over the wine, ritual hand-washing, the blessing over the bread, and the blessing after the meal.

IN THE SYNAGOGUE

The festivities of Simchat Torah begin in the evening with the *Maariv* service. After the recitation of the *Amidah*, the *hakafot* (Torah processionals) are begun with the recital of *ata hareita*, a collection of biblical verses in praise of God and the Torah. Each verse is read by the reader and then repeated by the worshipers in the congregation. In some communities each verse is read by a different member of the congregation and then repeated by the entire congregation.

After the recitation of the *ata hareita*, all of the Torah scrolls are removed from the Ark and carried in procession in the synagogue. This is done seven times, and in each procession each Torah is given to a different person so that as many people as possible should have an opportunity to participate. In traditional settings, all *kohanim* and *leviim*—priests and Levites—are honored first, followed by Israelites. Each procession is done to the chanting of prescribed hymns. To these are added songs and hymns of a joyous nature. Children, too, are invited to participate, often carrying specially created smaller Torah scrolls. It is also customary to hand out flags for children to carry, supposedly reminiscent of the tribal flags under which the Israelites marched in the desert. Another custom is to put an apple on top of the flag, or an apple with a hole carved out for a lighted candle—again, to evoke images of Torah as light.

It is considered a great honor to carry a Torah scroll, and everyone who is capable enjoys the opportunity to participate. Dancing in the synagogue sanctuary is often an important part of the festive processions as well, and in some synagogues the scrolls are carried out of doors, adding a wonderful spiritual dimension to the festivities.

After the seven *hakafot*, all of the Torah scrolls are returned to the Ark except for one. Custom varies about what is read on the night of Simchat Torah. In some places any portion that the scroll happens to be rolled to is read. The more traditional prevailing custom is to read *Vezot HaBeracha* (Deuteronomy 33), allowing three *aliyot*. Then the Torah is returned and the service is concluded.

Simchat Torah Morning

The morning service is the usual holiday one, with its own *Amidah* and the *Hallel* Psalms of Praise. After *Hallel* the *hakafot* processionals follow as on the night before. After the *hakafot*, all the Torah scrolls except three are returned to the Ark. Three scrolls are needed, one for the reading of the *sidra* of *Vezot HaBeracha*, the second for the reading of the first chapter of the Book of Genesis, and the third for the concluding *maftir* portion. Since the custom is for everyone to be honored with an *aliyah* on Simchat Torah, the section from *Vezot HaBeracha* is read over and over again. To facilitate this, large congregations will divide into smaller groups, each with its own Torah. Other congregations will call up more than one person at a time.

Usually the last *aliyah* is a special one, reserved for *kol ha-ne'arim*—"all the children." Only this one time during the year, children who have not reached the age of *Bar* or *Bat Mitzvah* are given a Torah honor. A large *tallit* is spread like a canopy over their heads as they say the blessings along with an adult who accompanies them.

The last part of the Torah reading from the first Torah scroll is the reading of the last verses of the Book of Deuteronomy (33:27–34:12) The person honored with this *aliyah* is called the *chatan Torah*—"groom of the Torah." In synagogues that are egalitarian and offer equal participation to women, a woman may be given this honor, called the *kallat HaTorah*—"bride of the Torah." This person is generally a distinguished member of the congregation, and is called up to the Torah with a special *piyyut* in praise of the Torah. The following is a suggested text for the calling up of the *chatan Torah*:

> Requesting permission of God, mighty, awesome, and revered, and requesting permission of the Torah, our precious treasure which we celebrate, I lift up my voice in song with gratitude in praise of the One Who dwells in sublime light, Who has granted us life and sustained us with faith's purity, Who has allowed us to reach this day of rejoicing in the Torah which grants honor and splendor, life and security, which brings joy to the heart and light to the eyes, and happiness to us when we incorporate its values which we cherish. The Torah grants long days and strength to those who love and observe it, heeding its warnings absorbed in it with reverence and love without setting prior conditions. May it be the will of the Almighty to grant life, lovingkindness, and a crown of blessings in abundance to _____ who has been chosen for this reading of the Torah at its conclusion.

After this *aliyah*, the beginning of Genesis (1:1–2:3) is read from the second Torah scroll. The person honored with this *aliyah* is called the *chatan Bereshit*—"groom of Genesis" (or *kallat Bereshit*—"bride of Genesis"). Again, a special *piyyut* is recited. As the first chapter of Genesis is read, the congregation recites for each day of creation *veyehi erev veyehi voker*—"there was evening and there was morning"—which is repeated by the Torah reader. It is customary in many places to spread a *tallit* like a canopy over the *chatan Torah* and *chatan Bereshit*.

The lifting of the second Torah scroll is done in a

special fashion. The person crosses his or her hands so that the scroll, when lifted, is reversed (i.e., the Hebrew script is facing the congregation). This is done to symbolize turning the Torah back to its beginning—to Genesis.

The third scroll is the *maftir* scroll, from which the concluding Torah portion of Numbers 29:35–30:1 is read. This is followed by the chanting of the Simchat Torah *Haftarah*, from the first chapter of the Book of Joshua.

Following is a summary of the Torah readings and *Haftarah* for Simchat Torah:

First Torah Scroll (Deuteronomy 33–34:12): These chapters bring to a close the Five Books of the Torah. They describe the final poem of Moses and the report of his death on Mount Nebo. Before Moses goes up to the mountain to have a brief look at the Promised Land before dying, he blesses the Tribes of Israel. Though they be separate tribes, Moses reminds them that they had been united together at Sinai where God revealed the Torah and where Israel, by accepting the Torah, entered into an eternal covenant with God. At the conclusion of the Torah portion, Moses ascends Mount Nebo and is presented with an overall view of the Promised Land. He then dies and is buried in the Valley of Moab and his grave remained unmarked forever. Israel mourns his passing deeply and now turns to his successor, Joshua, for leadership.

Second Torah Scroll (Genesis 1:1–2:3): The creation of the world in six days and the cessation of God's work on the seventh day is the theme of the reading from the second scroll on Simchat Torah.

Third Torah Scroll (Numbers 29:35–39): This scroll, from which the concluding *Maftir* portion is read, deals with the special burnt offering related to the eighth day of solemn assembly.

Haftarah for Simchat Torah (Joshua 1:1–18): The *Haftarah* tells of God's charge to Joshua, the successor of Moses. Joshua proceeds to carry out his leadership responsibility and tells the Israelites of his strategy for defeating the Canaanites. In turn, all of the Tribes of Israel pledge their loyalty to Joshua.

Musaf Additional Service

The *Musaf* Additional Service for Simchat Torah is the usual festival one, except that the joyous mood is maintained by the ingenuity of the reader. Latitude is given to merriment, and some synagogues allow tasteful "fooling around" in order to heighten the great joy of the day. Simchat Torah thus gives expression to the unbreakable chain—the Torah—that links past and future generations. In that chain lies the secret of the eternal validity of the Jewish people.

NOTABLE SUKKOT AND SHEMINI ATZERET QUOTATIONS

1. Rabbi Levi said: "The person who observes the precept of the *sukkah* in this world will be rescued by God from all loss and damage (*Otzar Midrashim*, ed. Eisenstein, p. 493).

2. Just as a person cannot fulfill his duty on Sukkot unless the four species are held together, so, too, the children of Israel cannot be redeemed unless all Israelites hold together (*Yalkut* 188a).

3. The palm branch resembles the spine, the myrtle is like the eye, the willow is like the mouth, and the *etrog* is like the heart. In this way we praise God with all of our limbs (*Yalkut* 188b).

4. When Rav Humnuna Saba entered his *sukkah*, he would stand at the door on the inside and say: "Let us invite the holy guests" (*Zohar* iii, 103).

5. Rabbi Yochanan said: "We wave the *lulav* to the four sides of the horizon, upwards and downwards, to demonstrate that God is everywhere" (Talmud, *Sukkah* 37b).

6. This is my God and I will glorify Him (Exodus 15:2). Rabbi Ishmael says: "Is it possible for a person of flesh and blood to add glory to His Creator? It simply means: I shall be beautiful before God in observing the commandments. I shall prepare before God a beautiful *lulav*, a beautiful *sukkah*, and beautiful phylacteries (*Mechilta de Rabbi Ishmael, Shirata* 3).

7. The *etrog* has a fragrance and a taste that is symbolic of those in Israel who possess an abundance of Torah and *mitzvot*. The fruit of the palm has no fragrance but has taste, symbolic of those scholars who perform only a few kind deeds. The myrtle has a fragrance, but no taste, symbolic of kindly persons who are unlearned. The willow has neither taste nor fragrance, symbolic of those persons who are neither learned nor kind. God says: "It is impossible for Me to destroy them, but let them all unite, and let each atone for the other" (*Yalkut Emor, Pesikta Buber*, p. 185).

8. On the first day of Sukkot, thirteen bullocks were sacrificed; on the second, twelve; on the third, eleven; on the fourth, ten; on the fifth, nine; on the sixth, eight; on the seventh, seven; a total of seventy. On Shemini Atzeret only one bullock was sacrificed. The seventy were brought to atone for the seventy nations of the world, and the one, for the nation of Israel.

Why were less sacrificed every succeeding day? To show that the number of nations persecuting Israel will become less and less, if his sins shall grow less (*Zohar*, iv, 476).

9. Rabbi Abin said: "Why did God require us to take the palm branch and the *etrog* on Sukkot? It is like two men who appeared before the king of judgment. The actual trial is held in secret. How do we know who receives the king's approval? If we see one of them depart with a palm branch in one hand and one beautiful fruit in another, we know that he has won.

"Likewise, we Jews, with the nations of the world, go before God on Rosh Hashanah and Yom Kippur, that our actions may be judged.

"How do we know who wins the approval of the King of Kings?

"Those whom God has enjoined to take up the palm branch and the *etrog*" (*Pesikta Buber*, p. 180).

10. If Hillel observed the Israelites in a mood of frivolity rejoicing in the joy of the drawing of water, he would say: "We are assembled here for what purpose? Does God need our praises if they be rendered in this mood? Has God not angels without number to praise Him?" But if he beheld the Israelites rejoicing in an earnest mood, he would say: "If we are not here to sing God's praise, who else could please Him as much? Does God not enjoy our praises more than the praise of His Heavenly Hosts?" (Jerusalem Talmud, *Sukkah* 5).

11. Rabbi Eliezer said: "A Jew should eat fourteen meals in the *sukkah*." King Agrippa's secretary objected,

saying: "But I cannot eat more than once a day." Rabbi
Eliezer said: "Every day you eat many appetizers for your
own sake, cannot you eat an extra appetizer at a time
different from your regular meal, for the sake of God?"
(Talmud, *Sukkah* 27).

12. The verse says: "You shall dwell in booths" and
continues "All shall dwell in booths" (Leviticus 23:42).
Rabbi Abba said: "The first part applies to the holy
guests, and the second to all Israel."

As for the Holy Guests, when Rav Humnuna Saba
entered the *sukkah*, he would stand at the door on the
inside and say: "Let us invite the holy guests." He then
made ready the courses, stood up, recited the *Kiddush*,
and continued: "Be seated, O guests of truth, be seated."

He then lifted up his hands and said: "Gracious is our
lot, gracious is the lot of Israel. Gracious is the lot of
mankind, who have been privileged in this. Gracious is
the lot of the righteous in this world and in the world to
come" (*Zohar* iii, 103).

13. There are four things taken up on Sukkot. Two of
them, the palm and the *etrog*, bear fruit. The two others,
the myrtle and the willow, bear no edible fruit. But all of
them are needed to observe the commandment. In a like
manner, when Israel fasts and prays for God's aid in the
hour of calamity, those who study the Torah and observe
the commandments, and those who are unlearned and
fail to observe the commandments, must unite in prayer
and fasting if they wish God to answer them (Talmud,
Menachot 27a).

14. On Shemini Atzeret God says: "You shall have a shutting off" (Numbers 29:35). But on Passover God says: "Shall be a shutting off to God" (Deuteronomy 16:8). Why these different expressions? God says to Israel: "On Passover shut Me off from giving rain to the land of Israel, but on Shemini Atzeret I shall shut you off, by My rains, from walking in My outdoors" (*Yalkut Hadash*, 188b).

15. I love the *mitzvah* of *sukkah*, for a man can enter with his whole body, even with the mud adhering to the soles of his boots (Baal Shem Tov).

16. When the Chassidic Rebbe Rabbi Mordecai of Lechovitz would enter his *sukkah* on the first night of the holiday, he would fall to the ground of the *sukkah*, kiss it, and sigh: "How dare a flesh-and-blood body tread upon such a beloved *mitzvah* as *sukkah*?"

17. In the time to come the Holy Blessed One will make a *sukkah* for the righteous from the skin of Leviathan. The rest of Leviathan will be spread by the Holy Blessed One upon the walls of Jerusalem, and its radiance will shine from one end of the world to the other (Talmud, *Baba Batra* 75a).

18. Some people maintain that they see the *ushpizin* guests in their *sukkah*. I say, however, that I believe that the *ushpizin* guests come to my *sukkah*. Faith is clearer and more certain than seeing (Rebbe of Kotzk).

SUKKOT AND SIMCHAT TORAH GAMES

1. FISH

Purpose: To review information related to Sukkot.

Group: Ages 4–9.

Time: 15 minutes.

Materials:
1. A magnetic fishing pole, made from a stick with string and magnet attached.
2. Paper fishes with paper clips attached.

Instructions:

1. Divide the players into teams.
2. Paper fishes, each with a Sukkot question written on it, are spread on the floor. (See samples.)
3. Give each player an opportunity to catch a paper fish with the magnetic fishing pole.
4. When a fish is secured, the player reads the question.

5. If the team to which the player belongs answers correctly, it receives the point value on the back of the fish. (*Note:* Each fish has a different point value, ranging from 1 to 3.)

6. If the question is answered incorrectly, the other team may answer the same questions. If both teams are incorrect, the fish is discarded and the next player on team 1 fishes for a question.

7. After all the fish are caught, the team with the most points wins.

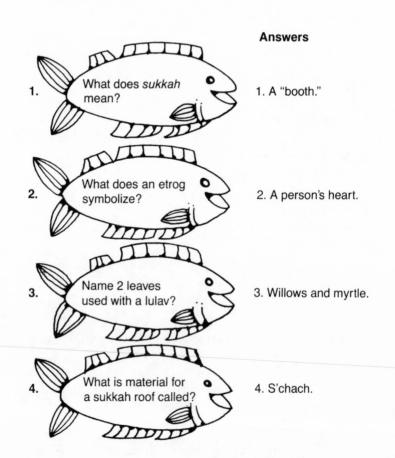

Answers

1. A "booth."

2. A person's heart.

3. Willows and myrtle.

4. S'chach.

2. BASEBALL GAME

Purpose: To afford players the opportunity to review their knowledge of Sukkot.

Group: Ages 6 and up.

Time: 20–30 minutes.

Materials: Questions related to the Sukkot holiday.

Instructions:

1. Divide the players into two teams.
2. "Pitch" to the first team by giving them a question related to Sukkot. If the player answers correctly, he goes to a spot in the room designated as first base. The next player who responds correctly goes to first base, and the first player moves to second base, and so on, until reaching "home." Each player who answers incorrectly is designated as "out."
3. Like the game of baseball, three outs terminate the inning. When the first player reaches home, he scores one run.
4. The team with the most runs at the end of a designated number of innings wins.

Variation:

1. Draw markings for tic-tac-toe on a flannel board. X's and O's are prepared on flannel backing.
2. Ask a Sukkot-related question. If the player an-

swers correctly, he puts his team's mark in the place of his choice. If incorrect, the question is asked of the opposing team. If neither team answers correctly, a new question is asked.

   3. The first team to make tic-tac-toe either across, down, or diagonally is declared the winner.

3. MATCH GAME

Purpose: To review facts and information related to Sukkot.

Group: Ages 8 and up.

Time: 30 minutes.

Materials:
   1. Index cards.
   2. Black markers.
   3. Sukkot-related questions with the last word omitted.

Instructions:

   1. Of the entire group of players, choose two to be the players for points. The others are designated as the panelists.
   2. Each player in turn is read a statement related to Sukkot, with the last word omitted; for example, my favorite part of owning an *etrog* is that it has a _____ . (*Note:* It is important that the statements are designed for more than one possible answer.)

3. Before each player reveals his answer, each of the panelists are asked to write their answers on index cards. After they have written their answers, the group leader asks the first player to declare his answer to the fill-in-the-blank statement.

4. For every match that a player makes with a panelist, 1 point is received.

5. Each player in turn is given an opportunity to hear a statement and match his answer with those of the panel.

6. The player with the most points wins.

4. SUKKOT LOTTO

Purpose: To practice reviewing facts related to Sukkot.

Group: Ages 6 and up.

Time: 30 minutes.

Materials:

1. An 8½ inch by 11 inch piece of paper ruled in 16 squares, each depicting pictorially or naming a Sukkot concept. (See sample.)

2. Paper markers to cover the squares.

Instructions:

1. Read from the list of Sukkot statements (see sample below). Pictures may be shown instead of reading the statements.

2. Each time a statement or picture corresponds to a square on a player's card, that player covers the square with a paper marker.

3. The first player to cover any four squares in a row either across, down, or diagonally is the winner. (Verification of the squares is established by the group leader after a "lotto" has been established.)

The following statements are to be used by the group leader. The numbers next to each statement are not to be read. They are merely to illustrate the correspondence of the Sukkot statements to the squares of the sample lotto card.

1. Picture of what you shake on Sukkot.

2. The English name for the leaves that symbolize a person's mouth.

3. The covering on top of the *sukkah*.

4. Picture of a citron.

5. The Hebrew word for "willow leaves."

6. The English translation of the word *sukkah*.

7. The date on which the festival of Sukkot occurs.

8. The Hebrew word for "palm branch."

9. The blessing over the *lulav*.

10. The duration in days of the festival of Sukkot.

11. The English translation of *etrog*.

12. Special prayer said the day after Sukkot.

13. Ceremony where ancient biblical guests are invited into the *sukkah*.

14. The symbolism of the palm branch.

15. The name in English for the *lulav, etrog*, and their leaves.

16. A *sukkah* is pictured like this.

1	2 Willow	3 S'chach	4
5 Aravah	6 Booth	7 15 Tishre	8 Lulav
9 Al nitilat lulav	10 8 days	11 Citrus	12 Prayer for Rain
13 Ushpizin	14 Spine	15 4 species	16

5. WORD SCRAMBLE

Purpose: To identify scrambled words related to Simchat Torah.

Group: Ages 10 and up.

Time: 20–30 minutes.

Materials:

1. Words related to Simchat Torah written on 5 inch by 7 inch index cards.

2. A watch with a second hand.

Instructions:

1. Divide the players into two teams.

2. Hold up the first scrambled word for both teams to see.

3. The first player to raise his hand and correctly identify the word receives 1 point.

4. If no player is able to identify the word after twenty seconds, a new word is shown to both teams.

5. The team with the most words identified wins.

Sample Words

1. OTRHA   TORAH

2. GNIGNIEBN   BEGINNING

3. FAAHKTO   HAKAFOT

4. SLGAF   FLAGS

5. NIGCIOJER   REJOICING

6. HOT POTATO

Purpose: To enjoy Hebrew music while manipulating a ball.

Group: Ages 5 and up.

Time: 15–20 minutes.

Materials:
1. A beachball.
2. List of Simchat Torah songs.

Instructions:

1. Ask the players to form a circle.
2. The group leader begins to sing a Simchat Torah song while a beachball is quickly passed around the circle from hand to hand.
3. When the singing stops, the player holding the ball is eliminated. The ball then continues to rotate as the music starts again to a new song.
4. The game continues. The last person in the circle wins and is afforded the opportunity to be the singer of the songs in the next round.

7. NAME THAT NIGGUN

Purpose: To review one's knowledge of Hebrew songs, particularly those related to Simchat Torah.

Group: Ages 8 and up.

Time: 30 minutes.

Materials: List of songs.

Instructions:

1. Divide the players into two teams.

2. Call the first players on each team to stand next to the group leader.

3. Sing the first three notes of the song to be identified.

4. The player on the first team is given ten seconds to name the title of the song. If correct, he receives a point. If incorrect, the player on the other team is given a chance to guess. If neither player can correctly identify the song, the group leader must sing the song again, this time adding one additional note to the three already sung. This procedure continues until one of the players is able to correctly identify the song. (*Note:* A maximum of seven notes is allowed to be sung by the group leader.)

5. The team with the most songs identified wins.

8. SIMCHAT TORAH ALPHABET SONG GAME

Purpose: This is another game to review Hebrew songs.

Group: Ages 10 and up.

Time: 30 minutes.

Materials: None.

Instructions:

1. Divide everyone into teams.

2. Ask each team in turn to sing a song beginning with a different letter of the Hebrew alphabet, beginning with

the first Hebrew letter, *aleph*. As long as a team sings a song beginning with the correct letter, that team remains in the game. Once a team fails to sing a song, it is eliminated.

3. The last team remaining wins.

SHORT STORIES

1. THE *HOSHANA* OF RABBI EPHRAIM

by D<small>AVID</small> E<small>INHORN</small>

The endless Russian plains stretch as far as the eye can see. Here and there a lake dots the landscape, with lush, green grass fringing the water's edge. In olden times, scattered villages nestled in the hills and dales bordering the lakes.

Once, a Jewish village lay sprawling near just such a lake. To get to the water, one walked a short distance from the town, climbed a sloping hill, and there it was—its surface like a gleaming mirror reflecting the deep blue of heaven. The horizon was unbroken save for one old willow tree whose drooping branches swayed in eternal mourning. Occasional drops of water fell from the branches like tears and made rippling circles in the still water. To the Jews of the village the tree became known as "Ephraim's *Hoshana*."

Many years ago (said the old folks) a wealthy man lived in the village. He had an only child, a brilliant boy named Ephraim.

His schoolmates called him "the curious dreamer" because he asked so many questions and because he spent whole summer days at the lake, lost in daydreams.

Each Sukkot his father would assign a task to Ephraim, a duty that the boy considered a great honor.

In those days of primitive transportation, an *etrog* and *lulav* were very expensive. They had to be brought from far overseas, and only the wealthiest people could afford them. Those who were fortunate enough to own an *etrog* and *lulav* considered it a *mitzvah* to lend them to the poor so that they might pronounce the blessing.

Every morning, Ephraim made his rounds with the *etrog* and *lulav*. First he went to the old yeshiva teacher, Rabbi Isaiah, who lived with his wife in a little village. Rabbi Isaiah was too feeble to get about much, and he could always be found poring over a holy book.

Rabbi Isaiah and Ephraim had become fast friends. The old man was the only one to whom the boy could confide his innermost thoughts.

"Your son will one day be a great rabbi," the teacher often said to Ephraim's father.

Once, when Ephraim brought the *etrog* and *lulav* to Rabbi Isaiah, the old man's attention was drawn to the lad's troubled expression. "What is it, my boy?" said the rabbi.

"Nothing," said Ephraim. "But . . . I just cannot understand the meaning of the *etrog* and the *lulav*, the myrtle and the willow branches."

"My child," answered the rabbi, "you know the explanations our sages have given us."

"I know," said Ephraim, "but I'm still puzzled."

"Well, then," said the rabbi with a smile, "perhaps you

will like my explanation. The *lulav* is a palm leaf. A palm tree reaches skyward and its leaves are like hands outstretched to heaven in prayer. The *etrog* has a delicate fragrance, and good deeds, say our sages, have the aroma of rare spices.

"The myrtle twigs, my child, represent beauty and modesty. The Hebrew word for myrtle is *hadassah* and that, as you know, was Queen Esther's name, for she was very beautiful. But it is also said that when Adam was driven from the Garden of Eden because he ate from the tree of knowledge, he took with him a myrtle branch. Later he planted it. It flowered beautifully, and when Adam looked at it, he dreamed that one day the whole world would be a Garden of Eden. We, too, wait and hope for the Messiah."

"And what about the willow branch . . . the *hoshana*?" asked Ephraim. "Why do we mistreat it so? At the morning service on Hoshana Rabbah, we beat the poor willow against the floor until all its leaves are gone! And didn't our ancestors hang their harps on the willows of Babylon because they were in exile? The willow has followed us everywhere."

"Yes, my child," said the rabbi. "It is a sign of our sadness and our longing. When we dream of being freed from exile, we thrash the symbol of our exile."

"I like the poor willow best of all. It is sad and lonely . . . like me." Ephraim's voice broke.

Rabbi Isaiah leaned over and said softly, "Bring three *hoshanot*—three willow branches—tomorrow. I will bless two with the *etrog* and *lulav*. The third I will bless separately and you will plant it near your favorite spot at the lake. Then we shall see what happens."

Ephraim did as he was bidden.

Years passed. Ephraim became a renowned rabbi. Isaiah died. And the little twig that the boy had planted blossomed into a great willow with massive branches and thick leaves. Rabbi Ephraim forgot all about his talk with Rabbi Isaiah. Nor did he know how the old teacher had blessed the third *hoshana*.

Then one day Emperor Napoleon marched into Russia with his armies. Soldiers in strange uniforms appeared. They blocked the roads and ordered the inhabitants of the little village to stay indoors.

Now it happened that Ephraim had gone to a wedding in a town an hour away from his home. He had decided to return on foot. Dusk had fallen when he reached the outskirts of his village. Suddenly he heard a sharp command, and he was startled to see armed men, shouting orders in a language he did not understand, pointing rifles threateningly at him.

Panic seized Ephraim and he began to run. With the soldiers at his heels he came to the little vale. A mysterious force seemed to spin him around, and against his will he panted up the sloping hill and down toward the lake.

Then something beyond belief happened. The dense foliage of the old willow tree parted and enfolded Ephraim like two protecting arms. Dumbfounded, he saw the branches weave themselves into a sheltering screen. When the French soldiers came charging up to the lake, they found no trace of a human being. The company commander snarled, "He couldn't have gotten through here. He'd need an axe to chop open a path. Probably ran to the village." And they left.

For two days and nights Ephraim remained in his hideaway. The long green willow leaves splashed raindrops into Ephraim's cupped palms, and he was refreshed. On the second day, sitting in silence in his shady shelter, Ephraim suddenly remembered his talk with Rabbi Isaiah. A tremor passed through him. This tree was the third *hoshana* that Isaiah had blessed and that Ephraim had planted!

No sooner had he remembered than the branches parted again. Ephraim saw the open path and knew that it was safe to return home.

To be sure, the French soldiers had departed. The villagers greeted Rabbi Ephraim joyfully. They had been certain that misfortune had befallen him.

The very next Sabbath, Ephraim came to the synagogue and recited *Gomel*, the blessing recited by those who are rescued from danger. In his sermon he recounted his talk of long ago with Rabbi Isaiah and described how he had planted the third *hoshana* that had so miraculously saved him from Napoleon's troops.

And he took a vow in the presence of the whole congregation. "Some day, God willing," he said, "I will journey to the Holy Land with my family. When I go, I will take with me a shoot of this willow and plant it near Jerusalem, so that the willow will be blessed to see the arrival of the Messiah."

"Who knows," he concluded, his voice trailing into a whisper, "perhaps branches of this very willow may one day grace the holy altar of our rebuilt Temple of God."

Translated from the Yiddish by Morris Epstein

2. THE COST OF AN *ETROG*

Nothing meant more to Nahum of Chernobyl than celebrating Sukkot with great joy. And nothing enhanced his joy like a lovely *etrog* from the Holy Land. But one year there was a drought in Israel, and there were very few *etrogim* available for the holiday. Only one man in Chernobyl had an *etrog*—Moshe Haim, the wealthiest man in town.

Desolate to be without an *etrog* for the holiday, Nahum decided that he must buy Moshe Haim's *etrog*. But he was a very poor man. What could he possibly offer Moshe Haim, the richest man in Chernobyl? The only things of value that Nahum owned were the Baal Shem Tov's *tefillin* that he had inherited from the Master. Surely he could not part with those! But how could he welcome the Festival of Joy without an *etrog*?

Then Nahum reached a decision. Seizing the *tefillin*, he ran to Moshe Haim's house and said to him, "I would like to buy your *etrog*!"

"You!" scoffed the rich man. "You could never afford it!"

Then Nahum held out the *tefillin*. "Would you accept these in exchange? They once belonged to the Baal Shem Tov."

Moshe Haim gasped when he saw what was in Nahum's hand. The holy Besht's *tefillin*!

"Very well," he said, trying to conceal his excitement. "I will sell you my *etrog*," and he placed the gleaming yellow fruit in Nahum's outstretched hand.

Overjoyed, Nahum ran home to show the *etrog* to his wife.

"Where did you get that?" cried his wife when she saw the *etrog*. "We don't even have enough food for the holiday!"

"I traded the Baal Shem Tov's *tefillin* for it," announced Nahum.

Enraged, his wife grabbed the *etrog* out of Nahum's hand and flung it to the ground, breaking off the *pittum* and thus making it unusable for the holiday.

Nahum's face flushed with anger, then suddenly grew calm. "Yesterday," he said, "we owned a priceless treasure—the Besht's *tefillin*. Today we owned another priceless treasure—a beautiful *etrog*. Now he have neither. But we still have each other. Let's not fight. Good *yomtov*!"

3. HOW K'TONTON PRAYED FOR RAIN

by SADIE ROSE WEILERSTEIN

K'tonton [a little Jewish Tom Thumb] rolled up his Simhat Torah flag and tucked it under his pillow—the wee Simhat Torah flag Father had made out of a bit of wood and a slip of paper. "Rejoice and be merry," said the little flag. How could anyone help being merry on a week so full of holidays? First came Sukkot, then Hoshana Rabbah. Tonight was Shemini Atzeret. Tomorrow night would be Simhat Torah.

"Mother," said K'tonton, "I'll surely go to synagogue on Simhat Torah, won't I?"

"Of course," said Mother, "if it doesn't rain."

If it doesn't rain! K'tonton hadn't thought about rain before. Suppose it DID rain! Suppose he could not go to synagogue and wave his flag. He looked anxiously out of the window. The sky was clear and cloudless, twinkling with stars. But you never could tell. A cloud might come up as big as a fist, and grow and grow.

All night K'tonton dreamed of clouds and storms, of wind and sweeping rain. He awoke to a pattering sound under his window. Rain!! But it wasn't rain. It was only the wind rustling the dried leaves on the *sukkah* roof.

Twice that morning during the synagogue service K'tonton forgot to say "Amen." He was so busy looking at the sky through the window. "It must not rain! It must not rain! It must not rain!" he kept whispering.

The cantor had gone out for a moment. He returned now dressed in a white robe, the same robe which he wore on Rosh Hashanah and Yom Kippur. K'tonton looked questioningly at his father.

"It's for *Geshem*, the prayer for rain," Father explained. "Have you forgotten?"

Geshem! The prayer for rain! K'tonton had forgotten. Soon all the congregation would be praying for rain. The cantor in his white robe would be praying for rain. He, K'tonton, would be praying for rain. But it must not rain. It must not!

The Ark was opened. The congregation arose. "Thou makest the wind to blow and the rain to fall." The cantor began his solemn chant.

> "Remember one who followed Thee
> As to the sea flows water!
> For Abram's sake send water!"

And all the congregation cried aloud, "For Abram's sake send water!" All but K'tonton. K'tonton shut his lips tight and made no sound. On and on went the cantor, and the people followed.

"For Isaac's sake send water!
For Jacob's sake send water!
For Moses' sake send water!
For Aaron's sake send water!"

Not a word did K'tonton say.

"For Israel's sake send water!" It was the last verse.

"Amen! Amen! Amen!" cried the congregation. K'tonton's mouth opened to form an Amen but he shut it quickly. It mustn't rain! He would not let it rain. The sky would be clear and he would go to synagogue and stand on Father's shoulder and throw kisses to the *Sifre Torah* and wave his flag. K'tonton looked defiantly at the sky.

But deep down in K'tonton's heart was something that had not been there before, something troubling and uncomfortable.

"Why, K'tonton, you haven't eaten a thing," said Mother at dinner as she looked at K'tonton's plate. It was piled high with chicken and *kugel* and carrot *tzimmes*. "Is anything wrong?"

"Nothing," said K'tonton. "I guess I'm tired. I'll take a little rest."

He climbed into his bed near the window. The sky was clear and cloudless. His wee flag crinkled comfortingly under his pillow, but K'tonton took no joy in the sky or in the flag. SOMETHING HAD GONE WRONG!

At last K'tonton slept. In his sleep he dreamed. He dreamed that he was in Eretz Yisrael, in the Land of Israel. But it wasn't a goodly land, a land of brooks of water and fountains that spring out of valleys and hills, a land of wheat and barley and vines and figs and pomegranates. It was a wasteland, a land parched and withered—a land that mourned. In this parched and barren land K'tonton heard the sound of prayer.

"Thou who causest the wind to blow and the rain to fall,
Send water!
Send water!
Send water!"

Startled, K'tonton looked about. It was the trees who prayed, the palm and the cedar, the olive and the citron, the myrtle, the willows of the brook. They rustled their withered leaves. They bowed and swayed. K'tonton saw that the tree that led in prayer was his own almond tree.

"Send water! Send water!" cried the almond tree. "For Israel's sake send water! For Israel's land send water!"

A sigh ran through its slender branches and set its dry leaves quivering.

Then a heavenly voice sounded in the still air. Two words spoke the heavenly voice.

"K'tonton shut his lips!
K'tonton would not pray!"

K'tonton awoke with a start and sprang from his bed. The little flag crinkled, but he pushed it firmly aside. He must pray for rain. He must pray at once. But how did one pray without a congregation? He remembered a story Father had told him. It was about Honi the Circlemaker. Long, long ago in the Land of Israel there had lived a righteous man named Honi. When the earth was parched and the springs dried up and no rain fell, Honi drew a circle on the ground. He stood in the center of the circle and cried to God for rain. And the rain fell.

K'tonton climbed quickly to his little grove on the windowseat. With his finger he drew a circle on the ground. He paused. Honi had been a righteous man and he was a sinner. But wasn't it written somewhere that if one were truly sorry and repented, he could stand even in the place of the righteous? No one, K'tonton thought, could be more full of repentance than he. He could feel the repentance in his throat, at his heart. He stepped firmly into the center of the circle and prayed.

"Thou who makest the wind to blow and the rain to fall,
For Israel's sake send water!
For Israel's land send water!
For my almond tree send water!"

He looked anxiously at the sky. A gray spot had appeared, a cloud as big as a fist. It grew. It spread. The whole sky turned leaden. A drop of rain splashed against the windowpane and came rolling down. K'tonton leaped into the air with a shout of joy.

That evening as K'tonton sat in his little grove watching the rain through the window and thinking of his almond tree—a green, fresh almond tree sucking up rain through its roots—he was interrupted by Father's voice.

"Where are you, K'tonton? Get your flag and hurry. We'll be late for synagogue."

"But the rain," said K'tonton.

"Never mind the rain," said Father. "I'll tuck you into my pocket."

4. HOW K'TONTON REJOICED AND WAS MERRY ON SIMHAT TORAH

by Sadie Rose Weilerstein

"Let me see your flag, K'tonton."

It was David who spoke. You remember David, don't you? The sick little boy who lived next door! He wasn't sick anymore. He was quite well now and came in often to play with K'tonton.

K'tonton [a little Jewish Tom Thumb] showed him his flag. It was a Simhat Torah flag. Father had made it out of a match stick and a slip of paper. There were golden lions on it and Hebrew words in beautiful tiny letters: "Rejoice and be merry on Simhat Torah."

But K'tonton wasn't merry. He wasn't the least bit merry. There was something in his heart that wouldn't let him be merry. K'TONTON WANTED TO BE BIG! As big as other boys—as big as David—big enough to march on Simhat Torah! K'tonton sighed. It was such a big, deep sigh that David jumped up in his seat.

147

"Goodness, K'tonton, what's wrong? It isn't Yom Kippur coming! It's Simhat Torah. Don't you like your flag?"

"Of course I do," said K'tonton. "It's a very good flag."

"Then what is the matter? We're friends, aren't we? You can tell a friend, can't you?"

So K'tonton told him. He told him all that was in his heart; how he wanted so much to march on Simhat Torah, and how he couldn't because he was too small.

"David," he said when he finished, "I was thinking—do you suppose I might happen to grow big enough by tomorrow? It says in the *siddur*, 'Thy miracles that are daily with us.' Daily is now, isn't it? And in the Bible it says, 'The low He makes high and the high He brings low'; and it says, 'Thy beginning shall be small, but thy end great.' It might happen, mightn't it?" He looked up eagerly at his friend.

"Y-e-s—it might," David said, "but I wouldn't count on it too much if I were you." Just then David's mother called him home.

"Better go to bed, David," she said, "you'll have to be up late tomorrow night."

So David went to bed, but he didn't sleep. Thoughts and verses kept running around in his head. Thoughts of K'tonton standing up on his father's shoulder watching the boys march by, when he wanted so much to be marching himself. Verses about "Miracles that are daily with us," and "The low He makes high," and "Thy end shall be great."

"He's GOT to march! He's got to!" thought David. "There must be a way." His forehead was puckered in thought.

Suddenly his face broke into a big smile. "I've got it!"

he said. "I've got it!" He turned over on his pillow and went to sleep.

Next day there was such whispering going on, in K'tonton's house. David whispered to K'tonton's father, and K'tonton's father whispered to David, and Mother whispered to both. But nobody whispered to K'tonton. I don't know why K'tonton didn't notice, but he didn't. Perhaps because he was too busy trying to be merry, when he didn't feel merry.

Night came at last and they all started out for the synagogue. David carried his big flag and K'tonton carried his little flag. Father didn't need a flag because he was going to carry a *Sefer Torah* and Mother didn't have one, because all that mothers do, is kiss the *Sifre Torah* and wave their hands. When they reached the synagogue the lights were all lit and the grown-ups were smiling and whispering. All the children were hurrying down the aisles with crinkly new flags.

"You'd better hurry, David," said K'tonton, "if you want a good place."

He was trying not to remember how much he wanted to march himself.

"Have to fix my flag first!" said David.

He sat down on a bench beside K'tonton and his father. K'tonton watched him carefully. First he took out of his pocket a big rosy apple with a hole in the middle. Then he stuck the apple into the stick at the top of his flag.

"I know what it's for," said K'tonton. "It's for a candle."

"Is it?" said Father, and the next minute he had picked K'tonton up and stuck HIM inside the apple, right in the hole in the apple where the candle belonged. K'tonton's feet fitted snugly inside. Then David lifted the flag with K'tonton at the top of it and hurried along the aisle. "The low He makes high," laughed David.

Oh, how astonished K'tonton was! On they went, straight toward the *bimah* with the brightly lighted candlesticks and the crowds of boys and girls.

"K'tonton! It's K'tonton!" called the children. "K'tonton will be our leader! Let K'tonton lead." They waved their flags so hard it sounded like the wind in the forest.

So K'tonton marched on Simhat Torah after all, high up on David's flag at the head of the line. The beautiful *Sifre Torah* were so near he could touch their velvet covers with his hand. Once, twice, three times, four times, five times, six times, seven times round they marched. High above them all, higher then the children, higher than the flags, almost as high as the *Sifre Torah* moved K'tonton waving his little flag.

"Rejoice and be merry on Simhat Torah."

5. GITA MEETS SOME FRIENDS

by Morris Epstein

Never was the synagogue so crowded. It was Simhat Torah eve. All the Torah Scrolls, clothed in their beautiful mantles, were taken out of the Ark. Around and around the synagogue they were carried—once, twice . . . seven times. Gita and Jerry and all the other pupils of the Hebrew school marched along with the grown-ups. They held high their little flags topped by shiny freckled apples.

The big people sang and clapped their hands and celebrated. Gita and Jerry paraded and ate the chocolate bars given out by the principal. Tomorrow night the holiday would be over. In the morning, the reading of the Torah would come to an end and would be begun all over again from the very first word: *"Bereshit."*

At last, the dancing and the singing drew to a close. Gita and Jerry went home with Mother and Father. When they got into the house, Mother looked at the kitchen clock. "My, it's *very* late," she exclaimed. "Into bed with you, Jerry and Gita."

The children undressed, washed, and brushed their teeth. They said their prayers with Mother and tumbled into bed. "I bet I'll be asleep in one minute," said Gita, yawning. "I bet I'll be asleep in one second," cried Jerry, curling up like a caterpillar.

But somehow, Gita couldn't find a comfortable spot. She tossed and turned. She rolled over and called softly, "Jerry!" But Jerry was fast asleep. Gita tried lying on her back, then on her stomach, and then on her side, but it was no use. She lay there a long, long time, staring into the dark. . . .

Suddenly she heard a faint scratch at the door. She sat up in bed and beheld a most amazing procession marching into the bedroom. First came a fat yellow *etrog*, with two twinkling eyes and a pair of stubby legs. Next strode a lanky *lulav*, with a long face and a pointy skull. He was followed by three myrtle twigs and two willow branches, rustling in a whispery sort of way. A cluster of five willow twigs, forming a *hoshana*, entered and curtsied to Gita. Brining up the rear was a stocky *sukkah*, which squeezed and huffed and puffed until it just managed to get through the doorway.

All the visitors formed a neat line and looked to the *sukkah* for a sign to begin. He nodded, and they all said, "Hello, little Gita!"

Gita was so startled that she had to open her mouth twice before anything came out. "Wh-what are *you* doing here?" she finally blurted.

"We're very sad," said the *lulav* with the long face.

"And we've come to make a request. But first, let us introduce ourselves."

"I-I know who you are," said Gita, rubbing her eyes in wonder. The visitors did not even seem to hear her and went right on talking.

"I'm the *sukkah*," said the stocky one in a deep voice. "I remind everyone of the forty years of wandering of the Israelites in the desert. After they left Egypt, you know, they lived in booths like me. And later, in Palestine, they built booths every Sukkot. They put twigs on me for a roof, so that they could see the stars in heaven shining through. And they decorated me with fruits and vegetables and thanked God for the fine harvest He had given to them. They brought the *lulav* in to me—"

"I'll speak for myself, thank you," broke in the lanky *lulav*. "Each day of Sukkot, I, a noble palm branch, am waved to the north, south, east, and west, to show that God rules everywhere. I am carried around the synagogue by all the men . . ."

"And so are we!" chimed in the fat *etrog* and the myrtle twigs and the willow branches. "We are the *hadasim* and the *aravot*."

"All of us, except the *sukkah*, represent the *Arbaah Minim*, the 'Four Kinds' of growing things," said the *etrog*. "I am like the heart, without which man cannot live. The *lulav* is the spine, the myrtle is the eye, and the willow leaves are lips. We declare that a human being ought to serve God with all his soul and body."

"Ho, there, what about me?" cried the cluster of five willow twigs. "I'm important, too! I'm the *hoshana*. On Hoshana Rabbah, people strike me on a bench till my leaves fall off. I remind them that just as leaves fall and grow again, so God always gives people life and new hope. And I want to say—"

"Stop! Stop!" cried Gita, holding her hands to her ears. "*I* know *who* you all are. I learned *all* about you in Hebrew school. And Daddy uses you, and . . . and . . . But, won't you please tell me *why* you are here?"

"Well, as my friend said," remarked the *sukkah*, "we have a request. Sukkot and Shemini Atzeret and Simhat Torah are almost over. Where shall *we* be the day after tomorrow? I, for one, will be demolished!

"Our request is—can't you please keep us with you?" pleaded the *sukkah*. "We want to stay all year round!"

"Yes!" all the visitors cried in a chorus. "*We want to stay with you!*"

"You poor things!" said Gita, full of sympathy for them. "I love you all! I'll take care of you. I'll take care of you! I'll . . ."

Suddenly Gita felt a hand shaking her. She opened her eyes and found Mother standing over her bed.

"Gita!" said Mother. "Wake up, dear. Why are you shouting so? It's morning. Jerry's been up for more than an hour. Don't you want to go to synagogue with Daddy?"

Gita blinked. The sun was streaming in through the window. Then she remembered her visitors. "Mother!" she cried. "What's going to happen to the *etrog* and *lulav* and everything after Sukkot?"

"Why," said Mother, "We'll take the *sukkah* apart and put it neatly into the cellar. We'll put the *etrog* into its soft nest of straw and Daddy will keep it along with the spices when he says the *Havdalah* on Saturday night.

And the *lulav* will stand tall and straight in the corner of the sun parlor."

"But—will they *like* that?" asked Gita. "Will they be happy?"

"What a strange question!" exclaimed Mother. "I suppose they will. They've done their job, and we have treated them carefully. I can't very will *ask* them though, can I?"

Just then, through the open bedroom door, Gita spied Father's tall *lulav*, standing in the corner of the sun parlor. A gust of wind blew in through the screened half-open window. And the lanky *lulav* rustled and quivered, his leaves scraping against each other, saying "Y-z-z, y-z-z, y-z-z!"

"Look, Mommy, look! The *lulav* is saying 'yes.' They will be pleased! They *really* will!"

Mother said, "Wonderful, dear. Now won't you get dressed?" And Gita did, thinking, "Golly, sometimes parents just *don't* understand the most important things of all."

6. THE MIRACLE OF THE MYRTLES

In the city of Tunis it was the custom of the Jews to erect their *sukkot* completely from myrtle. Soon after Yom Kippur they would go to the marketplace and buy for pennies bundles of myrtle branches that the Arabs would sell. But one year, on the day before Sukkot, all the Moslems joined together in raising the price of the myrtle to two *real*, an outlandish figure.

The Jews came to buy the myrtle and were asked to pay the new price. Most of the Jews, being poor, could not pay. They feared that perhaps they would have to celebrate the holiday without building *sukkot*, so they went to the house of their leader, Rabbi Chai Tayob, and told him about the new price of the myrtle and how they wouldn't be able to observe the *mitzvah* of *sukkah*.

Immediately, the rabbi himself went to the marketplace and approached one of the Moslems from among the sellers of myrtle. He asked the price of a bundle, and the seller answered, "Two *real*!" "Fine," the rabbi said, "but on the condition that you carry the bundle upstairs.

156

I live on the fourth floor." The seller followed the rabbi, who went up the stairs to his house. However, the seller continued to walk, up and up, higher and higher, until behold! He hovered between heaven and earth. The people in the market saw a man flying over them, but they couldn't recognize him for he was so far away.

The matter reached the house of the Bey, the ruler of the land. His people told him that a man was flying in the sky. At once the Bey called for the Jewish rabbi, knowing that only he could do miraculous things. And when the Bey asked the rabbi why the man was hovering in the atmosphere, the rabbi answered, "Let him come and tell his story."

The rabbi whispered the ineffable name and, immediately, everyone saw the man fall down, downward, until at last he arrived in the Bey's courtyard. The ruler asked the man what had happened and who had made him fly. The seller told everything: "All the sellers of myrtle decided to raise the price of a bundle to two *real*. The old rabbi came and bought from me a bundle of myrtle and asked me to carry them to his house on the fourth floor. He went up the stairs, and I followed. But suddenly I noticed that I continued to walk, up, way up, into the sky's atmosphere, and that there was only a step between me and my death."

When the Bey heard these words, he answered slowly, "And why did you raise the price of myrtle this year? Go immediately to the marketplace and tell your friends to lower the price as it was before!" The seller kissed the Bey's hands, as well as those of the rabbi, and begged for forgiveness. At once he ran to the marketplace and told his friends what had happened.

The sellers lowered the price of myrtle as the Bey ordered, and the Jews immediately bought the myrtle and went to erect their *sukkot.* That year they celebrated the holiday with thanksgiving and with joy.

As told to A. Rabi by Rabbi J. Patosi (Tunis) (A. Rabi, *As Told by Our Forefathers*, vol. 3, story #24)

7. FOR THE SAKE OF *MITZVAH* OF THE *SUKKAH*

There is a story about a certain man who, although he was very poor, was careful to observe the *mitzvah* of building the *sukkah* and to use within it the four species that were needed. One year the fourteenth of Tishrei came and the man did not have money to buy either sticks for a *sukkah* or the four species. He was extremely worried. How would he observe the *mitzvah* of *sukkah*?

Finally, he decided to take one of the utensils from his house and sell it in the market. With the money he would buy wood for the *sukkah*. However, the money from this transaction would barely be enough to buy sticks for the whole *sukkah*, and so he approached one of the Gentiles who was selling sticks and bought from him only a small bundle. Among these sticks, he saw a thick and strong one that appeared to him to be somewhat old. It was short and resembled a cane. Curious, the Jew asked the Gentile the nature of the stick.

The seller said, "This stick served as a cane for my old father who died suddenly and left these sticks. When I took the bundle to sell, I bound this cane with it, so that it should not remain in the house; there the children would hit each other with it, just as my old father did when he was still alive."

The Jew took the sticks and hurried home. When he entered the yard, his wife called, "Please do me a favor and don't bring all the sticks into the *sukkah*. Leave me some with which to make a fire, so that I will still be able to wash the children's clothes before the holiday."

Immediately, the husband gave his wife the cane that was bound together with the smaller sticks, and said to her, "Use this cane, which is very thick, and you will be able to build a good fire."

The woman took the cane and put it into the oven to burn. After some moments she saw, to her surprise, several gold coins falling from the burning cane. A jeweled necklace fell out as well. The woman ran to call her husband and show him the treasure that had fallen to their lot.

"Truly," they said, "this withered cane served as a secret storehouse for the old man who died! How lucky that this marvelous treasure has come into our hands!"

At once the man ran and bought the four species as well as all the other items for the holiday. With the rest of the money he opened a business and became rich. The Jew continued to give charity to others, and he and his family lived in wealth and honor.

As told to A. Rabi by Rabbi J. Messas (Morocco) (A. Rabi, *As Told by Our Forefathers*, vol. 2, story #12)

8. THE EMIR AND ELIJAH THE PROPHET

A rich Jew who lived in one of the villages in Bucharia would erect each year on the holiday of Sukkot a very beautiful *sukkah*. He would decorate it with large and sumptuous rugs and bring into it magnificent dishes. The roof was adorned with fruits of the season. The man and his family wore special clothes for the holiday and sat together all the days of the festival, which they celebrated with joy and with song.

The rich man's *sukkah* soon became famous for it was, indeed, so unusually beautiful. The Emir who lived in that village visited the rich Jew every year in the beautiful *sukkah*, and he, too, got great pleasure from it.

One year the rich man erected his *sukkah* as usual. But, behold! Seven days of the holiday went by and the Emir didn't come—for he was away from the village at that time.

After the holiday, the Jews of the village took apart their *sukkot*. Only the rich Jew didn't hurry to take his apart, for he thought, "I will let my *sukkah* remain for

161

several more days. Perhaps the Emir will soon return and want to visit me."

A week passed—and the Emir did return to the village. "I will go and pay my friend, the rich Jew, a holiday visit," he declared.

So the Emir went to the rich man's house and there was received with joy and with song. The Jew took him into the *sukkah* and set before him refreshments and coffee. The Emir sat for a short while, looked about him, and felt neither pleased nor happy. His face was covered with the shadow of sadness. When the rich man saw the Emir's face, he got very frightened. "Perhaps I insulted the Emir's honor and that is why he is sad," he thought. The Jew asked, "My dear Emir, I notice that your face is not as it was before. What has happened?"

And the Emir answered, "Every year when I entered the *succah* I saw a handsome old man sitting at the table. But this year I didn't see him. I have searched the entire *sukkah*, but he is nowhere to be found. Who is he? And where has he gone?"

And the Jew answered, "The man you saw was Elijah the Prophet, who appears on Sukkot; this year you didn't find him because the holiday has already passed. But even on Sukkot not everyone can see Elijah; you merited seeing what others didn't see. My dear Emir, you are truly fortunate!"

As told by a Jew from Buchara. (A. Rabi, *As Told by Our Forefathers*, vol. 2, story #10)

9. THE CLEVER JUDGMENT

In a certain house there lived two families, one Jewish and the other Gentile. The Jew lived on the second floor, and the Gentile lived on the first. The Days of Awe passed, the holiday of Sukkot arrived, and the Jew built a *sukkah* on his porch and covered it with branches of palm and olive.

The Gentile saw the *sukkah* and was very jealous. And what did he do? On the first day of the holiday he went to the police station and told a lie. "The Jew has built a *sukkah* on his porch and caused a lot of dirt. When the winds come, the branches fly into my house."

The Moslem captain at the police station ordered one of his officers to bring the Jew at once. And when the Jew arrived, the captain asked sternly, "What did you do on your porch?"

The Jew answered, "I didn't do anything, sir. I did not build or break. We Jews have an old custom of erecting a *sukkah* out-of-doors, and since I have no other place to put it, I made use of my porch."

163

The police captain, a clever man, thought for a while. "I rule that you have built an illegal structure," he declared. "I set aside eight days time, beginning from today, in which you must tear down the building that you have erected. And know that if you don't destroy it within that time, I will bring upon you harsh penalties of fines and jail!"

The Jew returned home, happy, satisfied, and full of thanks. He and his family rejoiced during their holiday. The fact that they had to take their *sukkah* apart after eight days did not deter their joy even a bit.

As told by S. Hilles (Tunis) (D. Noy, *Jewish Folktales from Tunisia*, story #17)

10. THE BROKEN *PITAM*

A rich but ignorant Jewish villager became related by marriage to a poor but learned Jew. On the day before Sukkot, a time when Jews start buying *etrogim* and when those who are meticulous pay high prices for an *etrog* free of any blemish, the villager went and spent a large sum and asked that he be given a "beauty of beauties"— for he needed it as a gift for his relative, a pious and learned man. The ignorant man had heard that an *etrog* had to have a *pitam*, a protuberance on top. Without this, it was worthless and ineligible for a blessing.

Now, to be sure that the *etrog* reached his relative without damage, the man called his servant, Stefan, and said, "I hereby give unto your possession an expensive item, an *etrog* with a *pitam*. Woe be unto you if you lose the *pitam*. But if you guard it carefully, be assured that you will get a reward. Now take this 'beauty' and bring it to the nearby town where my relative lives."

On the way to the town, Stefan was afraid that maybe he would trip and fall and, thus, break the *pitam*. He thought of what to do to avoid this. He concluded, at last, that the best and wisest thing to do was to take off the *pitam* and hide it. And that is what he did! He removed the *pitam* and put it carefully into one of the pockets of his pants.

Soon afterwards, Stefan arrived at the town and placed the *etrog* into the possession of the relative. The latter opened the box, and, to his surprise, saw that the *pitam* had been removed. The man stood astonished, not knowing what conclusion to reach: Has his relative, being ignorant, not known what to buy and been fooled? Or was the relative, being rich, trying to make sport with him, a poor man?

While the man thus stood and wondered, Stefan removed the *pitam* from his pocket, showed it proudly to the relative, and asked, "Is it true that you are waiting for this? Behold, it was in my pocket, for I wanted to keep it safe!" And while saying this, he placed the *pitam* into the hand of the bewildered Jew.

As told to Z. N. Haimovits by H. Frankel (East Europe)

GLOSSARY OF TERMS

Aliyah The honor of being called to the Torah

Aravot The willow leaves that are attached to the *lulav*

Chag "The Festival," a name for Sukkot

Chag HaAsif "Feast of Ingathering," a synonym for Sukkot

Chatan Bereshit Special Simchat Torah honor of being called to the Torah for the reading of Genesis

Chatan Torah Special Simchat Torah honor of being called to the Torah for the reading of the Haftarah.

Etrog A citron, one of the four species used during Sukkot

Four Species The *etrog, lulav, aravot,* and *hadassim*

Hadassim The myrtle leaves that are attached to the *lulav*

Hakafot The honor of marching around with a Torah scroll on Simchat Torah

Hoshannot Prayers of salvation said during the festival of Sukkot

Hoshanna Rabbah The name given to the seventh day of Sukkot

Kittel White robe worn by the cantor during the prayer for rain on Shemini Atzeret

Kol Nanearim "All the children"; special Simchat Torah ceremony of having all children called to the Torah to recite a blessing together

Lulav Palm branch, one of Sukkot's four species

Sechach The green covering of the roof of the *sukkah*

Simchat Bet Hashoevah "The water-pouring festival" that used to be observed during the days of the Temple

Tefillat Geshem Prayer for rain in Israel, recited on Shemini Atzeret

Yizkor Memorial prayers for the dead

Zeman Simchatenu "Season of our rejoicing," another name for Sukkot

FOR FURTHER READING

Bloch, Abraham P. *The Biblical and Historical Background of the Jewish Holy Days*. New York: Ktav Publishers, 1978.

Epstein, Morris and Ezekiel Schloss. *The New World Over Story Book*. New York: Bloch Publishing Company, 1968.

Frankel, Ellen. *The Classic Tales*. New Jersey: Jason Aronson, 1989.

Ganzfried, Solomon. *Code of Jewish Law*. New York: Hebrew Publishing Company, 1961.

Gaster, Theordor H. *Festivals of the Jewish Year*. New York: William Morris and Company, 1953.

Golomb, Morris. *Know Your Festivals and Enjoy Them*. New York: Shengold, 1973.

Greenberg, Irving. *Living the Jewish Way*. New York: Summit Books, 1988.

Isaacs, Ronald H. and Kerry M. Olitzky. *Sacred Celebrations: A Jewish Holiday Handbook*. New Jersey: Ktav Publishers, 1994.

————. *The How to Handbook of Jewish Living, Volume 1*. New Jersey: Ktav Publishers, 1993.

Isaacs, Ronald H. *The Jewish Family Game Book for the Sabbath and Festivals*. New Jersey: Ktav Publishers, 1989.

Klein, Isaac. *A Guide to Jewish Religious Practice*. New York: Jewish Theological Seminary, 1979.

Strassfeld, Michael. *The Jewish Festivals*. Philadelphia: Jewish Publication Society, 1985.

Waskow, Arthur. *Seasons of Our Joy: A Handbook of Jewish Festivals*. New York: Summit Books, 1982.

INDEX

Apocrypha, Sukkot, 9–11

Babylonia, four species, 53
Beauty, four species, 50
Bible
    four species, 45–54,
        52–53
    Shemini Atzeret, 94
    sukkah, 54–55
    Sukkot, 3–7
Blessings, Sukkot, home
    celebration, 20–28
"The Broken *Pitam*"
    (short story), 165–166

"The Clever Judgment"
    (short story), 163–164
Cloud of glory, Sukkot, 68
"The Cost of an *Etrog*"
    (short story), 140–141

Customs and rituals,
    Sukkot, 20

Distress, *sukkah* and, 69

Einhorn, David, 135–139
"The Emir and Elijah the
    Prophet" (short
    story), 161–162
Epstein, Morris, 151–155
Etrog. See also Four species
    Sukkot, 19, 32, 67–68
    uses of, 70–71
Etrogim, 72

Flavius Josephus, 13
"For the Sake of *Mitzvah*
    of the *Sukkah* (short
    story), 159–160

177

Four kingdoms, four
     species, 53
Four species, 45–54. *See
     also Etrog; Lulav*
  assembly of, 53–54
  Bible, 45–54
  laws of, 46–50
  symbolism, 50–53
Fragrant children, Sukkot,
     67
Frankel, H., 165–166

"Gita Meets Some Friends"
     (short story), 151–155
Greece, four species, 53

Haftarah summaries,
     Sukkot, synagogue
     celebration, 33–34
Haimovits, Z. N., 165–166
Hakhel, Sukkot, 7–8
Hebrew letters, *sukkah*
     and, 66
Hilles, S., 163–164
Home celebration
  Shemini Atzeret, 95–96
  Simchat Torah, 104
  Sukkot, 17–31
     customs and rituals,
          20
     preparations, 17–20

"The *Hoshana* of Rabbi
     Ephriasm" (short
     story), 135–139
Hoshanna Rabbah
  shadow and, 70
  Sukkot, synagogue cele-
     bration, 37–42
  women's customs,
     67–68
Hoshannot, Sukkot, syna-
     gogue celebration,
     34–35
"How K'tonton Prayed for
     Rain" (short story),
     142–146
"How K'tonton Rejoiced
     and Was Merry on
     Simhat Torah" (short
     story), 147–150
Human body, four species,
     51, 52

Joy
  four species, 50
  Sukkot, 65

Kabbalah, Sukkot, 37
Kissing, *sukkah* and, 67

Land of Israel and, Sukkot,
     66
Leviathan, *sukkah* and, 70

Lubavitcher *Chassidim,*
    *sukkah*mobile, 69
Lulav. See also Four
    species
  life and, 53
  shake publicity, 72
  Sukkot, 19–20, 32

Maimonides, 50
Messas, J., 159–160
"The Miracle of the
    Myrtles" (short story),
    156–158
Mitzvah
  four species, 51
  of *Sukkah,* 68
Musaf Additional Service,
    Simchat Torah, 109

Persia, four species, 53
Pizza, Sukkot, 71–72
Prayer for rain *(Tefillat
    Geshem),* Shemini
    Atzeret, 97–100
Pregnancy, Sukkot, 67

Rabbinic literature, Sukkot,
    8–11
Rain
  prayer for *(Tefillat
    Geshem),* Shemini
    Atzeret, 97–100
  sukkah and, 69–70

Rituals. *See* Customs and
    rituals
Rome, four species, 53

Seventy oxen, Sukkot,
    65–66
Shadow, *Hoshanna
    Rabbah* and, 70
Shemini Atzeret
  Bible and Talmud, 94
  home celebration,
    95–96
  legends of, 75–89
  overview, 93–94
  quotations, 113–117
  synagogue celebration,
    96–100
Short stories
  "The Broken *Pitam,*"
    165–166
  "The Clever Judgment,"
    163–164
  "The Cost of an *Etrog,*"
    140–141
  "The Emir and Elijah
    the Prophet,"
    161–162
  "For the Sake of *Mitzvah*
    of the *Sukkah,*
    159–160
  "Gita Meets Some
    Friends," 151–155

Short stories (*continued*)
  "The *Hoshana* of Rabbi
    Ephriasm," 135–139
  "How K'tonton Prayed
    for Rain," 142–146
  "How K'tonton Rejoiced
    and Was Merry on
    Simhat Torah,"
    147–150
  "The Miracle of the
    Myrtles," 156–158
Simchat Torah
  games for, 121–131
  home celebration, 104
  overview, 103–104
  synagogue celebration,
    104–109
    morning service,
      106–109
    Musaf Additional
      Service, 109
Sukkah, 54–61
  Bible, 54–55
  construction of, 55–56
  design of, 60–61
  distress and, 69
  dwelling in, 56–58
  Hebrew letters and, 66
  mitzvah of, 68
  rain and, 69–70
  symbolism of, 58–60
  Talmudic debate, 70

Sukkot. *See also* Four
    species; *Sukkah*
  four species, 45–54
  games for, 121–131
  historical perspective,
    3–14
    Bible, 3–7
    hakhel, 7–8
    post-biblical writings,
      11–14
    rabbinic literature,
      8–11
  home celebration, 17–31
    blessings, 20–28
    customs and rituals,
      20
    preparations, 17–20
    ushpizin, 28–31
  legends of, 75–89
  oddities and curiosities,
    65–72
  quotations, 113–117
  sukkah, 54–61
  synagogue celebration,
    31–42
    Hoshanna Rabbah,
      37–42
    Hoshannot, 34–35
    intermediate days,
      36–37
    Torah and *Haftarah*
      summaries,
      33–34

Symbolism
  four species, 50–53
  sukkah, 58–60
Synagogue celebration
  Shemini Atzeret, 96–100
  Simchat Torah, 104–109
    morning service,
      106–109
    Musaf Additional
      Service, 109
  Sukkot, 31–42
    Hoshanna Rabbah,
      37–42
    Hoshannot, 34–35
    intermediate days,
      36–37
    Torah and *Haftarah*
      summaries,
      33–34

Talmud
  Shemini Atzeret, 94
  Simchat Torah, 103–104
Talmudic debate, *sukkah,*
  70

Tefillat Geshem (prayer for
  rain), Shemini Atzeret,
  97–100
Torah
  Simchat Torah, 103–104
  Sukkot
    festival names, 68
    synagogue celebration,
      33–34
Types of Jews, four
  species, 52

Ushpizin, Sukkot, 28–31

Water libation, Sukkot,
  9–11
Weilerstein, Sadie Rose,
  142–146, 147–150
Women's customs,
  Hoshanna Rabbah,
  67–68

Yannai, Alexander
  (Hasmonean king), 72
Yuchi Indian tribe, Sukkot,
  69

About the Author

Rabbi Ronald H. Isaacs has been the spiritual leader of the Temple Sholom in Bridgewater, NJ, since 1975. He received his doctorate in instructional technology from Columbia University's Teachers College. He is the author of more than sixty books. His most recent publications include *Every Person's Guide to Death and Dying in the Jewish Tradition* and *Every Person's Guide to Jewish Philosophy and Philosophers.* Rabbi Isaacs currently serves as chairperson of the publications committee of the Rabbinical Assembly of America and with his wife, Leora, designs and coordinates the adult learning summer experience called Shabbat Plus at Camp Ramah in the Poconos. He resides in New Jersey with his wife, Leora, and their children, Keren and Zachary.

RECOMMENDED RESOURCES

**Every Person's Guide to Death and Dying
in the Jewish Tradition**
by Ronald H. Isaacs   0-7657-6028-2

Every Person's Guide to Hanukkah
by Ronald H. Isaacs   0-7657-6044-4

Every Person's Guide to the High Holidays
by Ronald H. Isaacs   0-7657-6018-5

Every Person's Guide to Jewish Law
by Ronald H. Isaacs   0-7657-6115-7

**Every Person's Guide to Jewish Philosophy
and Philosophers**
by Ronald H. Isaacs   0-7657-6017-7

Every Person's Guide to Jewish Prayer
by Ronald H. Isaacs   0-7657-5964-0

Every Person's Guide to Jewish Sexuality
by Ronald H. Isaacs   0-7657-6118-1

Every Person's Guide to Passover
by Ronald H. Isaacs   0-7657-6043-6

Every Person's Guide to Purim
by Ronald H. Isaacs   0-7657-6046-0

Every Person's Guide to Shabbat
by Ronald H. Isaacs   0-7657-6019-3

Every Person's Guide to Shavuot
by Ronald H. Isaacs   0-7657-6041-X

Available at

your local bookstore
online at www.aronson.com,
or by calling toll-free 1-800-782-0015